DRAWING IS COOL

ARCTURUS

ARCTURUS

This edition published in 2011 by Arcturus Publishing Limited
26/27 Bickels Yard, 151–153 Bermondsey Street,
London SE1 3HA

Created by: Dynamo Limited
Cover design: Gary Sutherland and Akihiro Nakayama
Editors: Anna Brett and Kate Overy

ISBN: 978-1-84837-766-0
CH001682EN
Supplier 05, Date 0111, Print run 603

Printed in Singapore

Contents

Introduction

In this book you'll learn how to draw an amazing array of things. Our simple step-by-step technique will help you to create some fantastic images!

Just follow the steps . . .

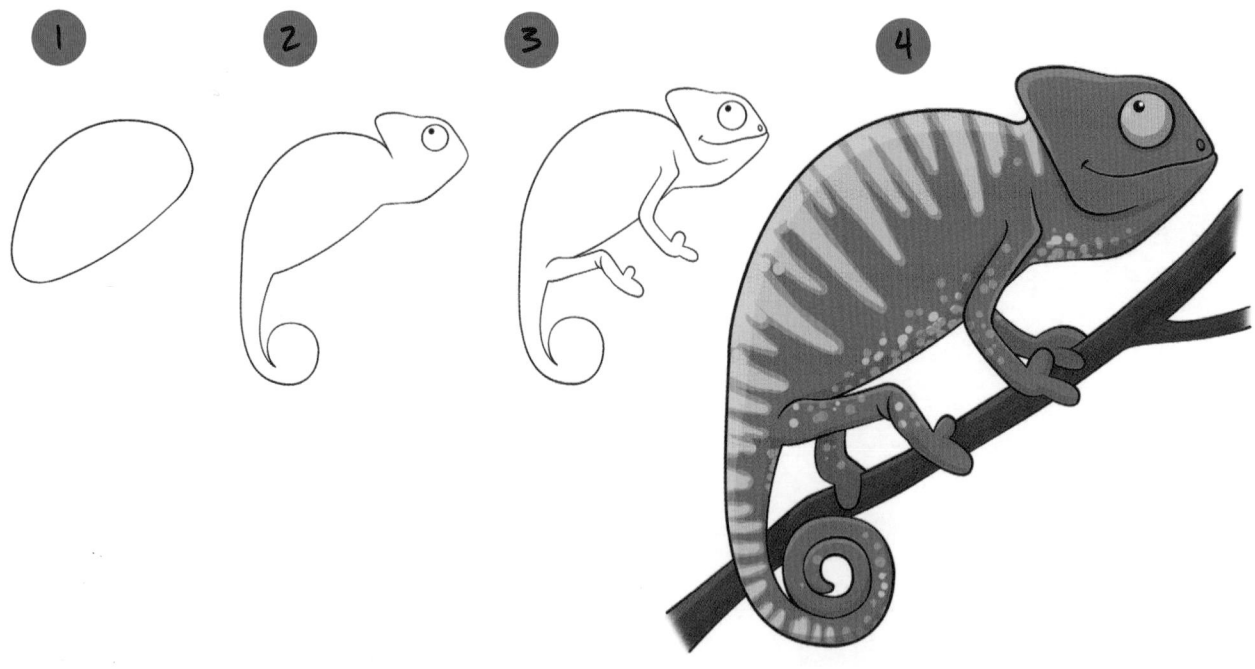

. . . and you'll be drawing like a professional in no time!

Materials

Before you start, there are some important things you need.

You can choose from a variety of drawing tools, including pencils, pens, chalks and paints. An ordinary HB pencil is best to start with.

You will need a clean sheet of paper for your final drawings, but scrap paper is useful for your practice work.

We all make mistakes once in a while – that's why every artist has a good eraser as an important part of his or her equipment.

There are many types of eraser available, but a nice soft one with a chisel tip is best to start with. When using your eraser, always be gentle and rub out the mistake gradually. Scrubbing hard at your paper will smear and ruin your work, and possibly even rip your drawing.

You can choose from a range of tools to create perfect shapes. A good, solid ruler is ideal for drawing straight lines.

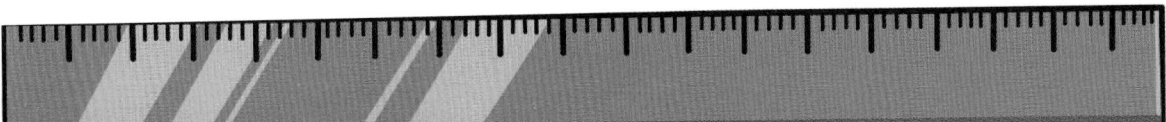

You can draw a perfect circle with a pair of compasses, but they can be tricky to use at first. Try using a coin, bottle top or any other small round item you can find.

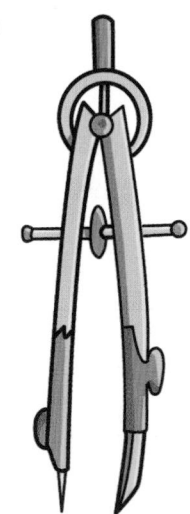

The drawings in this book have been finished with an ink line to make them sharper and cleaner.

Professionals use dipping pens and brushes, but you can achieve a similar effect by using a ballpoint or felt-tip pen.

First test your felt-tip on a piece of paper similar to the one you will be using for your final drawing. This way you can make sure the ink doesn't spread too much on the paper.

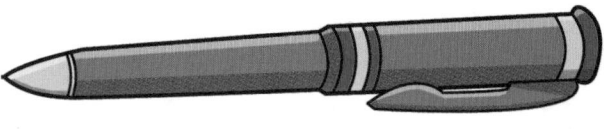

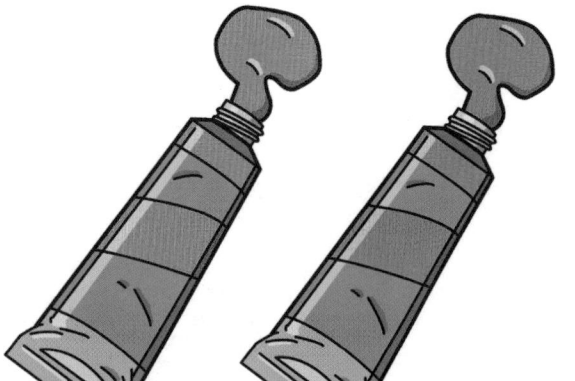

Adding colour to your drawing will really bring it to life.

Use water-based paints, like poster paint or gouache, as these are easier to clean out of your brushes or mop up after any spillages.

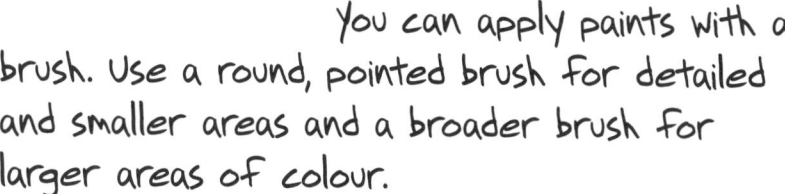

You can apply paints with a brush. Use a round, pointed brush for detailed and smaller areas and a broader brush for larger areas of colour.

Alternatively, you can use felt-tip pens or coloured pencils to colour your drawing.

Getting Started

Before you start, look at the finished picture you want to draw and think how it will fit on the page. Get an idea of its shape, position and size. Here we've used the spinosaurus from page 50.

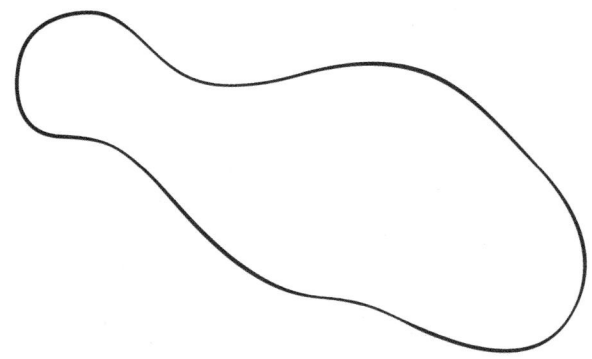

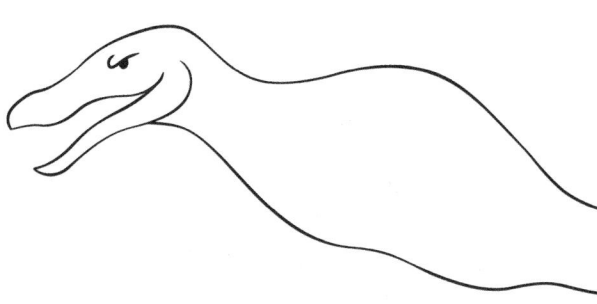

Look at how the parts fit together to make the final image. It's important to note where the lines end. Try to make sure they don't run outside the shape.

Once you are happy that the basic shape is correct, you can start using your pencil to add in the detail.

Next ink over your pencil line and then, once it's dry, gently rub out the line with your eraser. Finally, add your colour and your drawing is finished!

You don't have to copy just the pictures in this book. Anything with a face can be given expression and character.

Practice altering the facial features to see what effect this has on your character. Look how you can change the expression of the prince from page 31 with just a few simple lines.

Grumpy   Happy   Cheeky   Tired

If you want to practice before making your final pencil drawing, lay a thin piece of paper on top of it so you can see the shape through it.

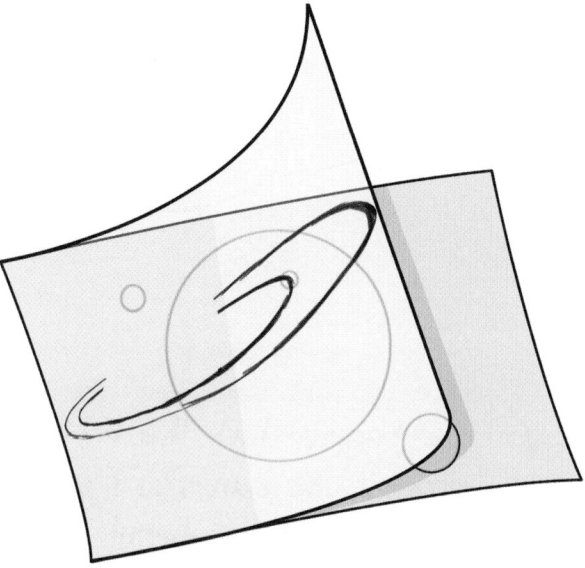

Try drawing different things on the top piece of paper. Now press down on it to see how the whole image looks.

Colour

When using colour, it really helps if you work steadily and don't rush. This is especially important if you are working with paints, as mistakes are more difficult to correct.

Apply the colour thinly at first, as this allows the white paper to shine through and makes the colour brighter.

 Using just one colour creates a flat image, as shown here.

 Adding a darker shade of the same colour makes your image look more solid and three-dimensional.

 If you want to add some highlights to your picture, simply use a lighter tint of the colour. Apply this to the areas where the light would naturally hit the image.

Try to use a different brush for each colour to avoid making your painting look messy. If you use a different brush for the darker and lighter colours, the latter will keep their brightness.

If you only have one brush, make sure you wash it out well before using a different colour.

Hints and Tips

Why not try combining two pictures to make a scene? Here's the cameraman from page 73 filming the sabre-toothed cat from page 58.

Alternatively, you can combine two similar images. For example, putting the sandcastle from page 109 with the shells from page 97 will make a beach scene.

What about giving your drawing a background? Paint a suitable scene, then either draw your character over it, or cut the figure out and stick it on top. Here's the pony from page 119 walking in a lovely green field.

Sea Creatures

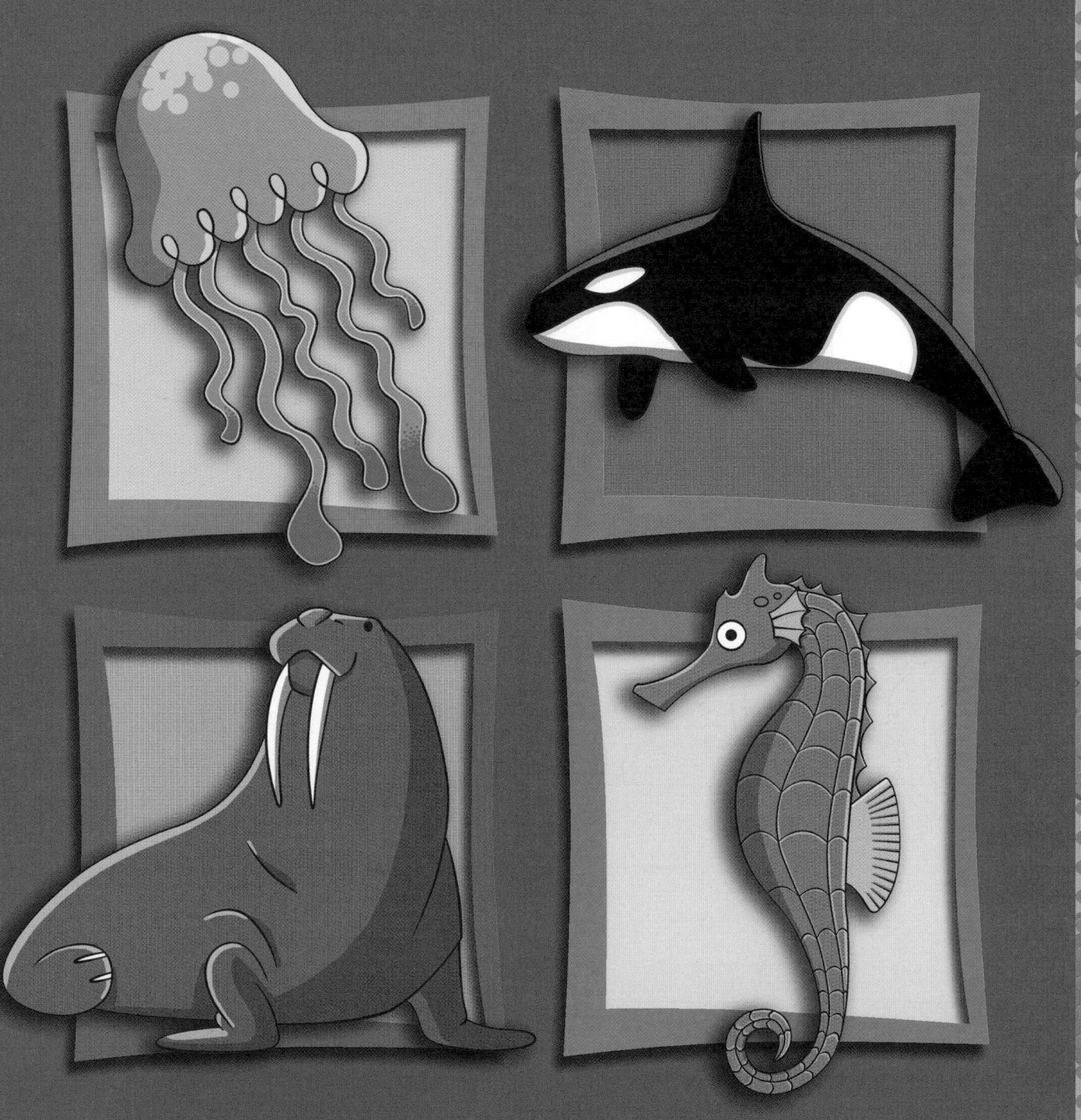

Clown Fish

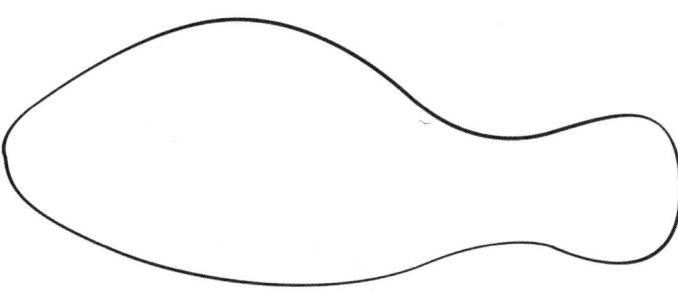

1. Begin with this fishy body shape.

2. Add the fins and a beady eye.

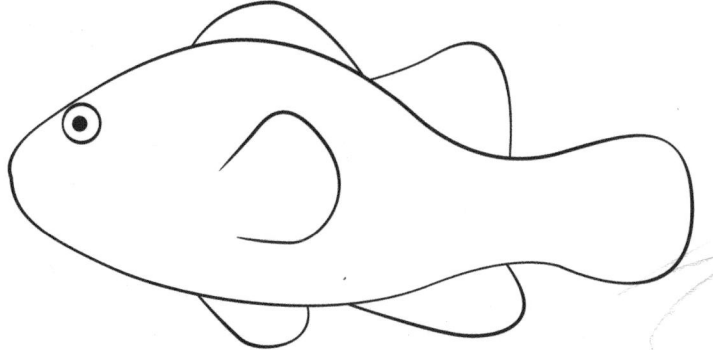

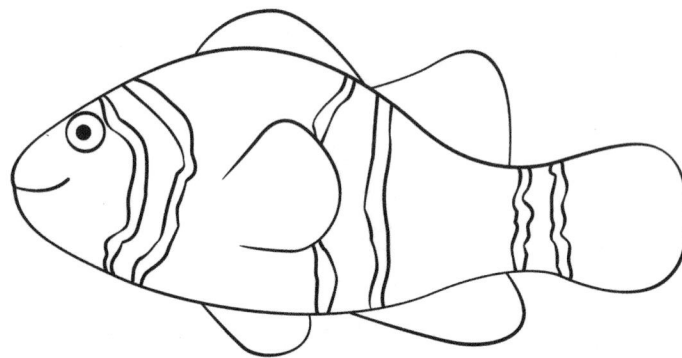

3. Draw some wavy lines for the stripes.

4. Draw some extra, thinner lines on the fins and colour the fish an eye-catching bright orange.

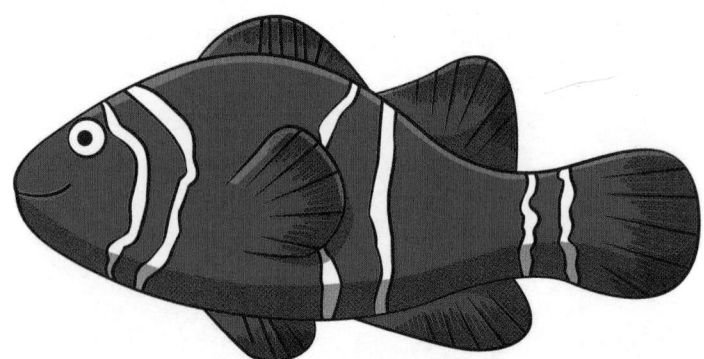

Turtle

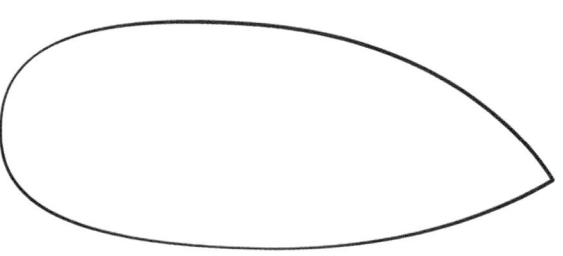

1. Start with a stretched egg shape.

2. Divide it in half to make the shell, then add the head.

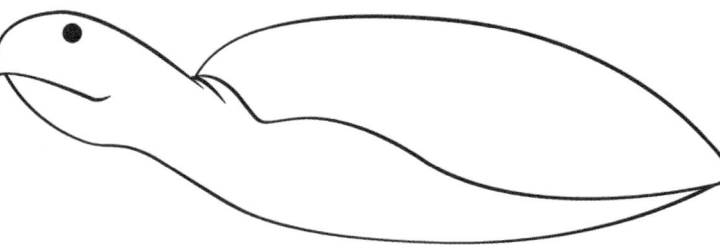

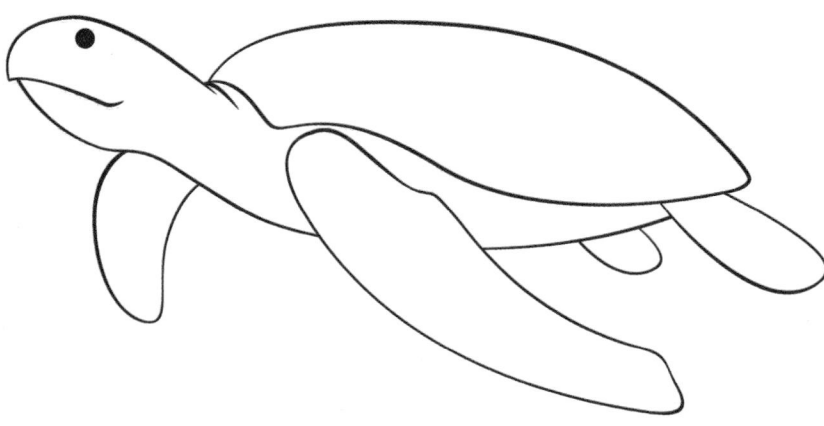

3. Add flippers to the front and back of the body.

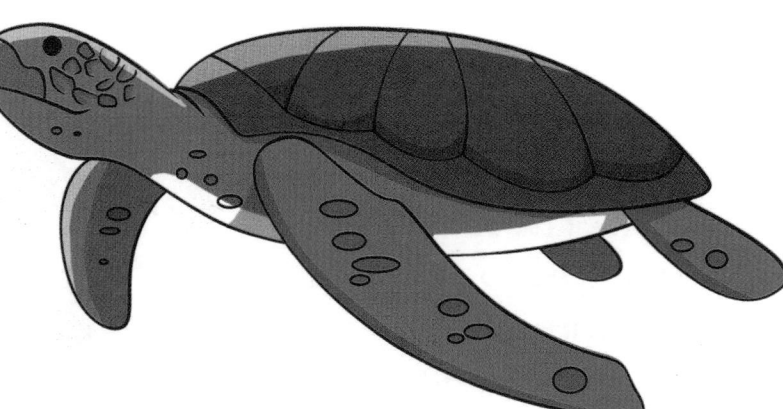

4. Add some spots to create his scaly skin, then colour him in.

Killer Whale

1. A long droplet shape makes up most of the body.

2. Draw in the tail and dorsal fin.

3. The front fins finish off the main shape.

4. Killer whales are unique in their appearance, so you need to follow the colouring of this example closely.

Seahorse

1. This strange, curved shape makes up the body.

2. Add the head with a long snout, and a curly tail.

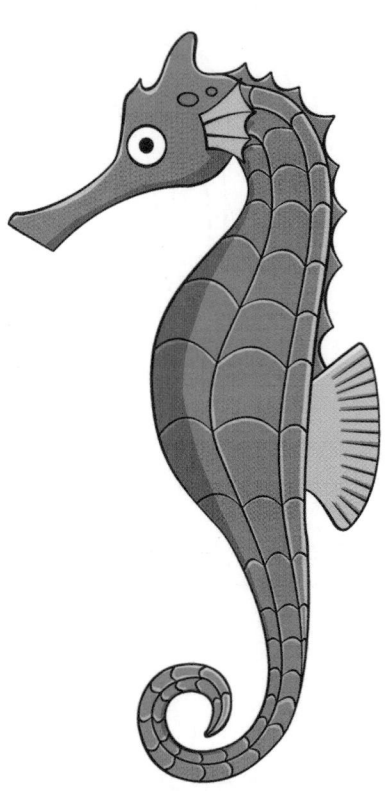

3. Draw fins on the head and the back to finish off the body.

4. Don't forget the spiky mane down the seahorse's neck.

Walrus

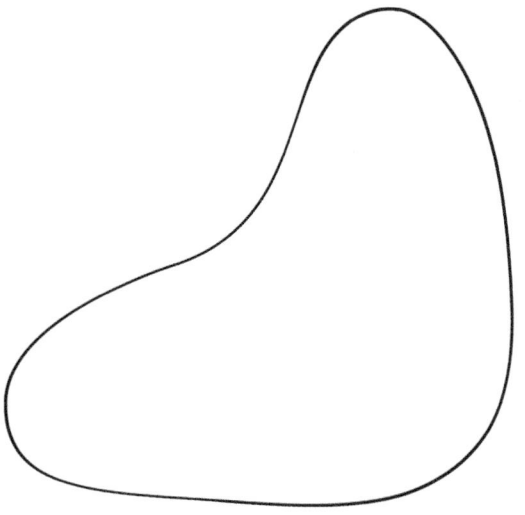

1. Draw a large blob for the body.

2. Add a round, smiling face.

3. Draw long tusks, a tail and a flipper at the front.

4. Draw in the other front flipper, and colour your walrus grey.

Narwhal

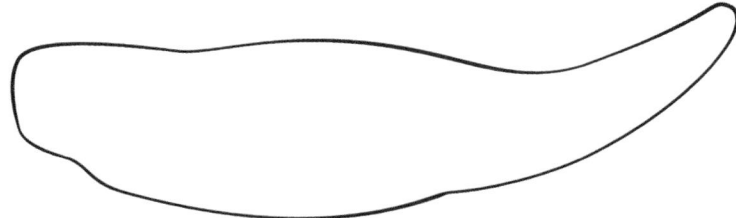

1. This simple shape is the starting point for this strange beast.

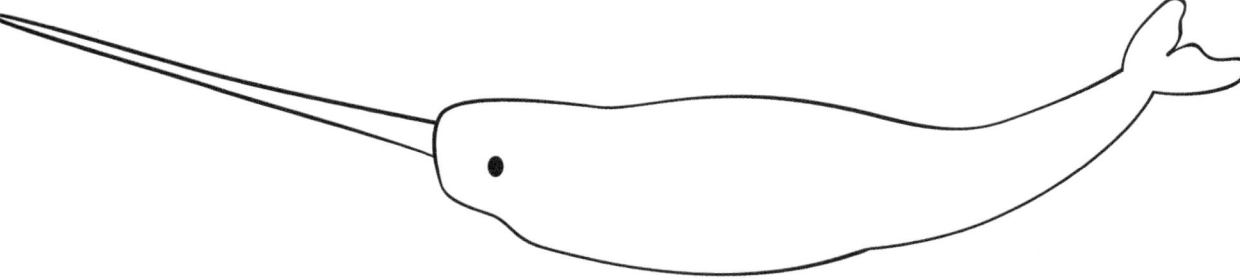

2. Add a long, pointed horn at the front, like a unicorn.

3. Simple fins and a smiley face are next.

4. Grey colouring finishes this drawing, although you could also colour him white, if you like.

Jellyfish

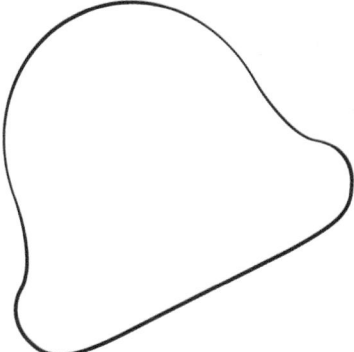

1. A basic bell shape creates the body.

2. Draw some curves along the bottom.

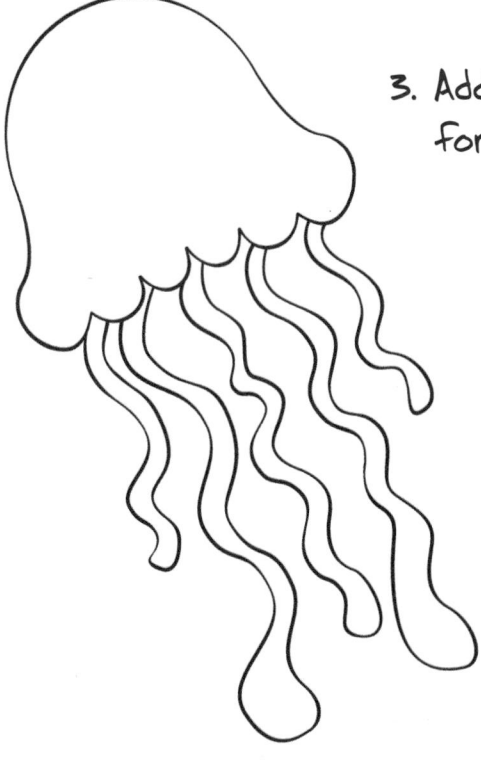

3. Add lots of wavy tentacles for catching prey.

4. Use as many colours as you like to finish off.

Sea Otter

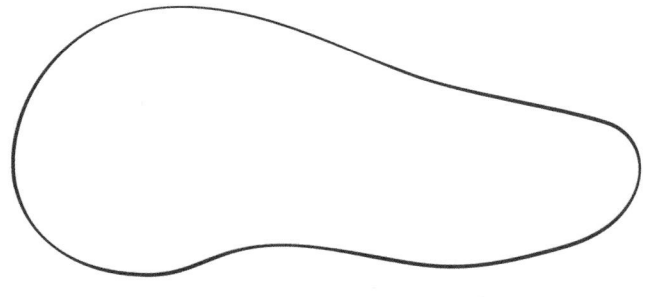

1. A squashed blob shape is the starting point.

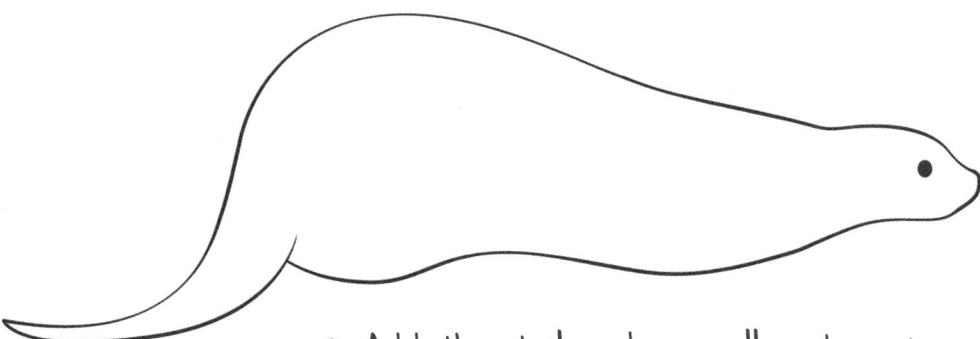

2. Add the tail and a small, cute eye.

3. This creature walks on stubby legs.

4. Make sure the otter's brown fur is darker on its back than on its belly.

Sailfish

2. Add a pointed tusk at the front and a wide tail at the back.

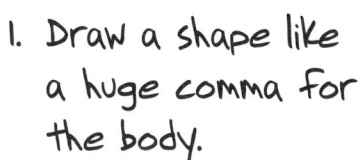

1. Draw a shape like a huge comma for the body.

3. This fish gets its name from the large sail-like fin on its back.

4. Use different shades of blue to colour in this fast swimmer.

Lobster

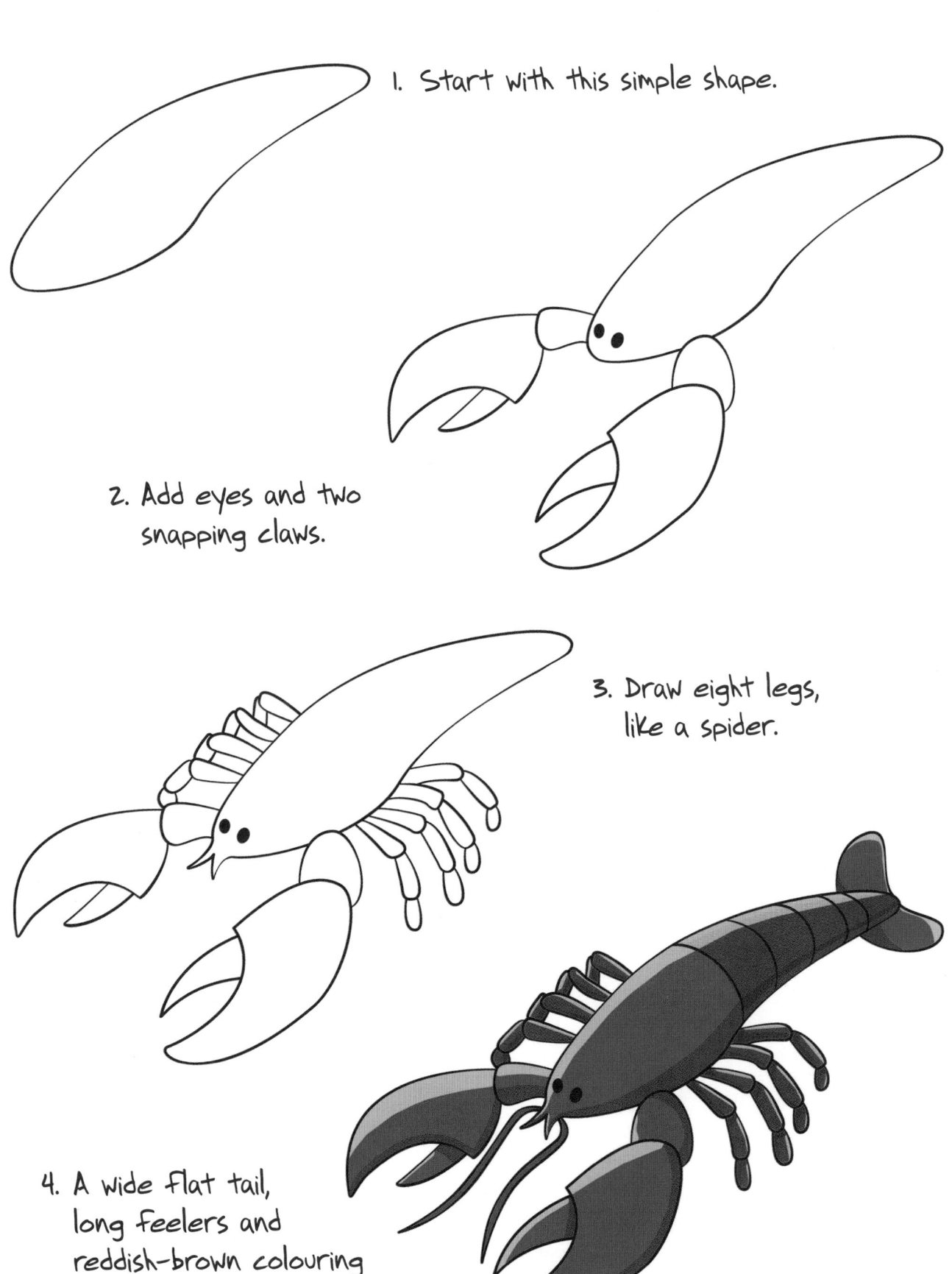

1. Start with this simple shape.

2. Add eyes and two snapping claws.

3. Draw eight legs, like a spider.

4. A wide flat tail, long feelers and reddish-brown colouring finish him off.

Hammerhead Shark

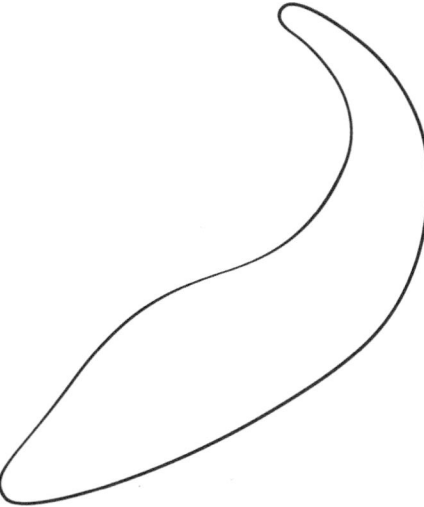

1. Draw a simple curved shape for the body.

2. Add a tail flicked out to one side and a hammer-shaped head.

3. Wide, flat fins make it look like a shark.

4. Use dark blue or grey colouring.

Octopus

1. A bulb shape with curly tentacles at the base starts the body.

2. Add two eyes and more tentacles.

3. Draw still more tentacles – you need eight in total.

4. Add suckers on the tentacles, then colour it in any way you want.

Sea Lion

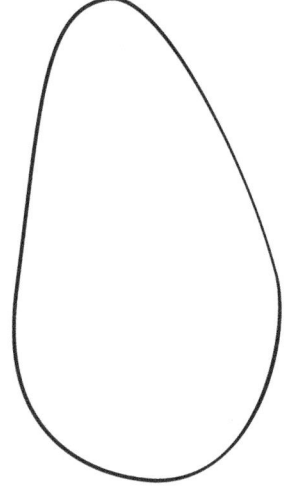

1. This squashed egg shape makes the body.

2. Extend the tail and add the head.

3. Draw two front flippers and the tail, then you are nearly done.

4. Colour him brown or grey. Don't forget to add the whiskers.

Anglerfish

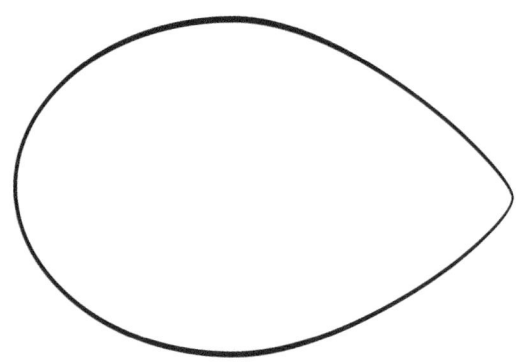

1. Start with an egg shape that's pointed at one end.

2. Anglerfish have large, round eyes and a huge mouth.

3. Add the fins and a fishing-rod type 'lure' on top of the head.

4. Add lots of fearsome teeth and then colour it in. Make the lure a glowing yellow for attracting prey.

Stingray

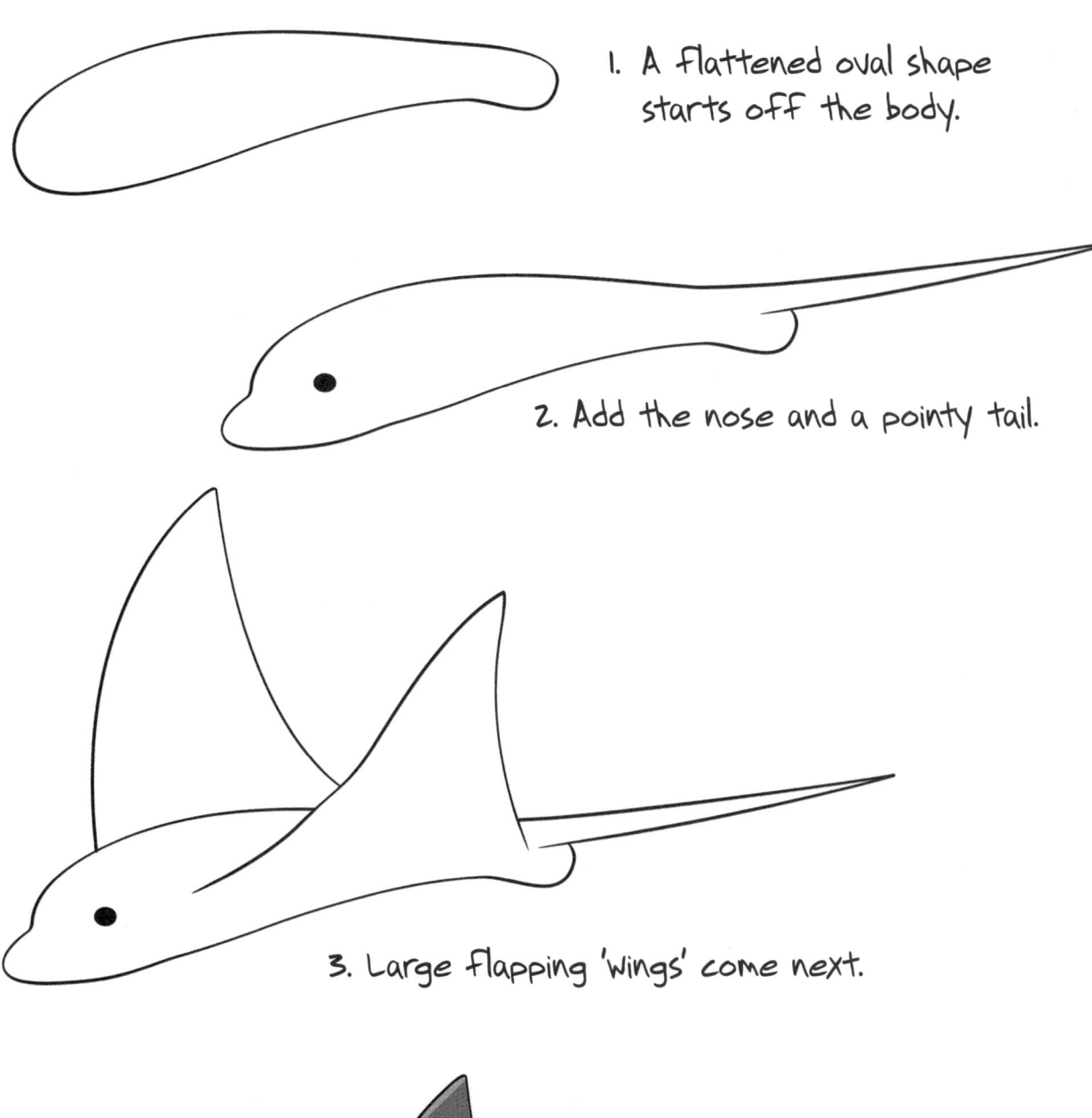

1. A flattened oval shape starts off the body.

2. Add the nose and a pointy tail.

3. Large flapping 'wings' come next.

4. Colour your stingray green, or greenish-brown.

Fantasy Figures

Angel

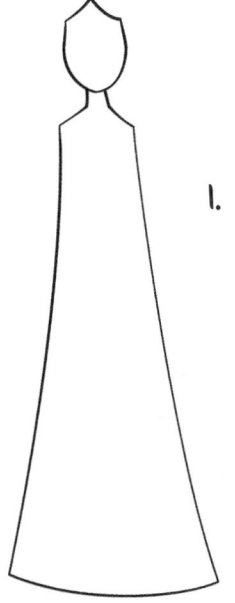

1. This long, thin bell shape forms the dress.

2. Draw the hands in a praying pose.

3. Add some large wings for heavenly flight.

4. Colour her in soft blue for a light, airy feel.

Goblin

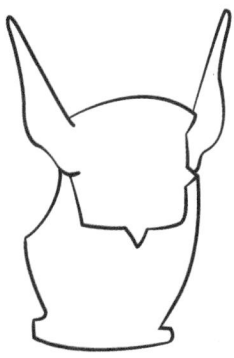

1. Draw this odd, spiky shape.

2. Add strong arms with gloved hands. Give him two mischievous eyes.

3. Now draw in his lower body and evil grin. Add boots for some bad-tempered stamping!

4. Goblins have green skin and horrible yellow teeth.

Princess

1. Start with this shape for the girl's head and upper body.

2. Add long hair and a pretty face.

3. Give her a flowing dress with a tight bodice and puffed sleeves.

4. Use light, bright pastel colours for your fairytale princess.

Prince

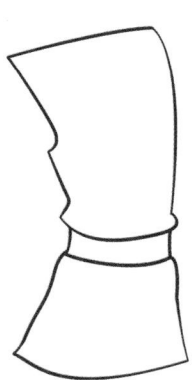

1. Draw this shape to create the top half of the body.

2. A strong chin and an upright pose tell you that he's a hero.

3. Add a cape and boots with cuffs for a fairytale princely touch.

4. Don't forget to include a crown, and a sword for slaying dragons.

Sorceress

1. Start with this shape for the upper body and head.

2. Add an open mouth and pointed eyebrows.

3. Add in a cloak and give her spiky hair.

4. Don't forget to add a dramatic flash and a long wand for powerful magic.

Wizard

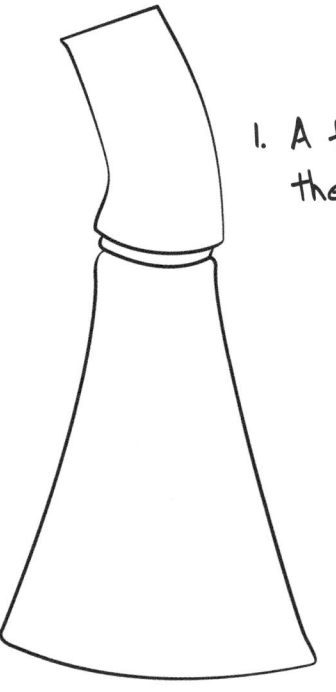

1. A flowing shape creates the impression of a robe.

2. Give him a long beard and pointy ears.

3. Draw his arms stretched out in front of him, as if casting a spell.

4. Draw the glowing magical light between his hands and use bright colours for his robes.

Water Nymph

1. Begin with the head and body. Remember to add a pointy ear.

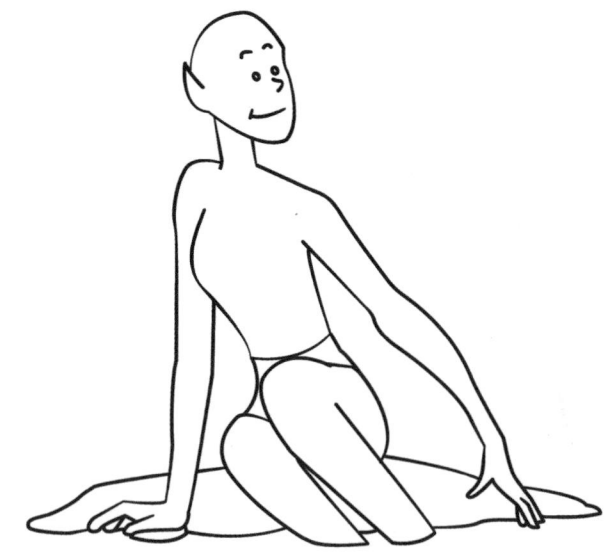

2. Add the arms and legs, and a rock for her to sit on. Keep your drawing light and delicate.

3. Give her some straggly, wet-look hair.

4. This nymph is green, but yours could be shades of blue.

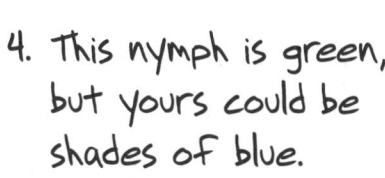

Knight

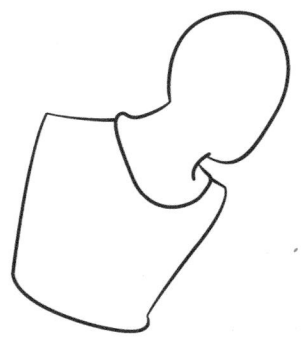

1. Start by drawing the head and body, using this shape.

2. Build up the arms using circles and rectangles. Give him a shield.

3. Add the legs, again using circles and rectangles. Draw in the grill on his visor.

4. Use shades of pale blue to create the impression of shiny metal. Colour the shield in heraldic red and yellow.

Pixie

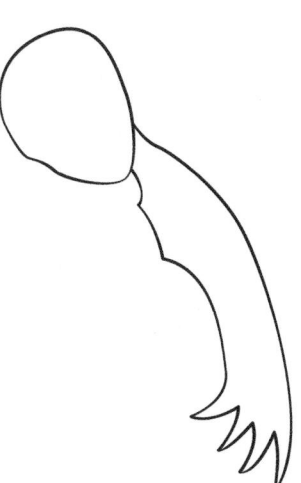

1. Draw a very slim body and an egg-shaped head.

2. Add large, pointy ears and a mischievous face.

3. Her arms should be thin, just like her body.

4. Long legs with spiky boots finish the outline. Green clothes complete this cheeky pixie.

Hobbit

1. Draw a round, heavy head and a plump body to match.

2. Hobbits aren't known for their tidy hair . . .

3. . . . but they are known for their hairy feet!

4. Colour him in earthy browns and greens. Add a torch for exploring dark caves.

Female Superhero

1. The upper body and flowing hair are the starting point.

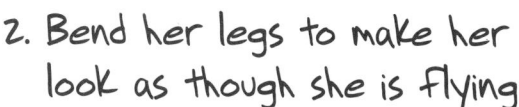

2. Bend her legs to make her look as though she is flying.

3. Draw her arm outstretched to make it look as though she is reaching out of the page.

4. Add movement lines for an action-packed pose. Colour her in bright blue and yellow for a comic-strip effect.

Male Superhero

1. Start by drawing the head, hair and upper body.

2. Add two arms. The flowing lines give lots of movement.

3. Use the same fluid lines for his legs.

4. Add zigzag lines around his hands to make it look as though he has just landed from leaping off a tall building.

Female Supervillain

1. An angular body is the starting point.

2. Add a square, bobbed haircut and a mean-looking face.

3. Long, thin legs make her look very tall.

4. Dark green and purple add to her sinister look.

Male Supervillain

1. A bulbous head and flowing body help to create the mad scientist look.

2. Give him a robotic arm. His other arm should have an angrily clenched fist.

3. A terrifying metal claw and a mask covering his face add to the scary look.

4. Add some squiggles to his head to make it look as though his brain is showing.

Warrior

1. Curved shapes make up the body and armour, while a rectangular shape creates his head.

2. Muscular arms and large hands make him look powerful.

3. Furry shorts and boots give him a wild, cave-man look.

4. Don't forget his swords and a shield on his back. You could give him a spear instead of swords.

Prehistoric Beasts

Woolly Mammoth

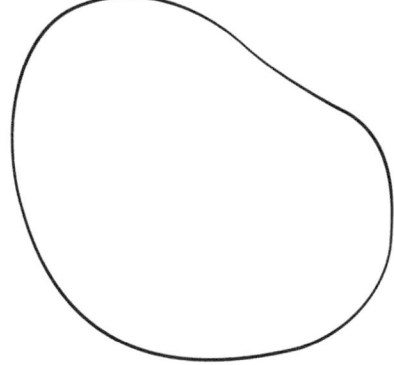

1. Use a squashed circle for the body.

2. Add the head and a long curling trunk.

3. Draw the two legs nearest to you – don't forget to make them woolly.

4. Complete the picture by adding two more legs and long, pointy tusks.

Glyptodon

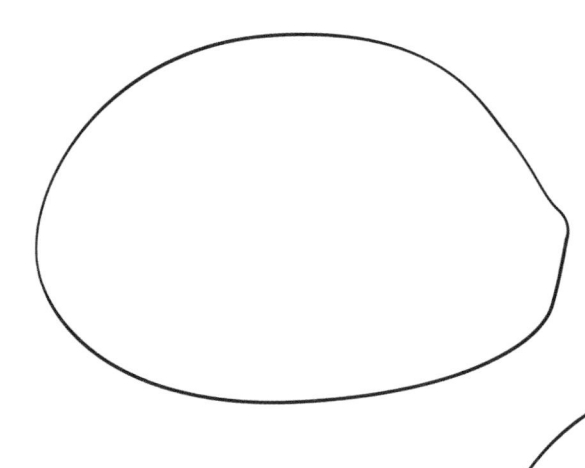

1. A squashed circle makes the glyptodon's body.

2. A short, fat pointy tail and chunky head are next.

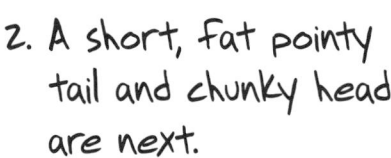

3. Everything about this creature is short and stocky, even the legs.

4. Finish it off by adding a solid shell. Draw sections on the shell and spikes on the tail to look like armour.

Ichthyosaur

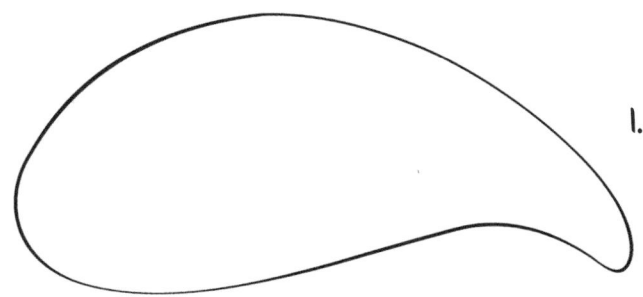

1. Draw a teardrop shape on its side for the body.

2. Add a long snout and pointy tail, just like a dolphin.

3. Add the flippers and a fin like a shark.

4. Draw one more fin at the back and colour him in.

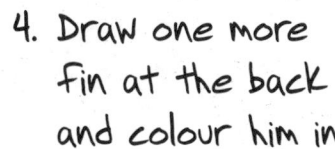

Allosaurus

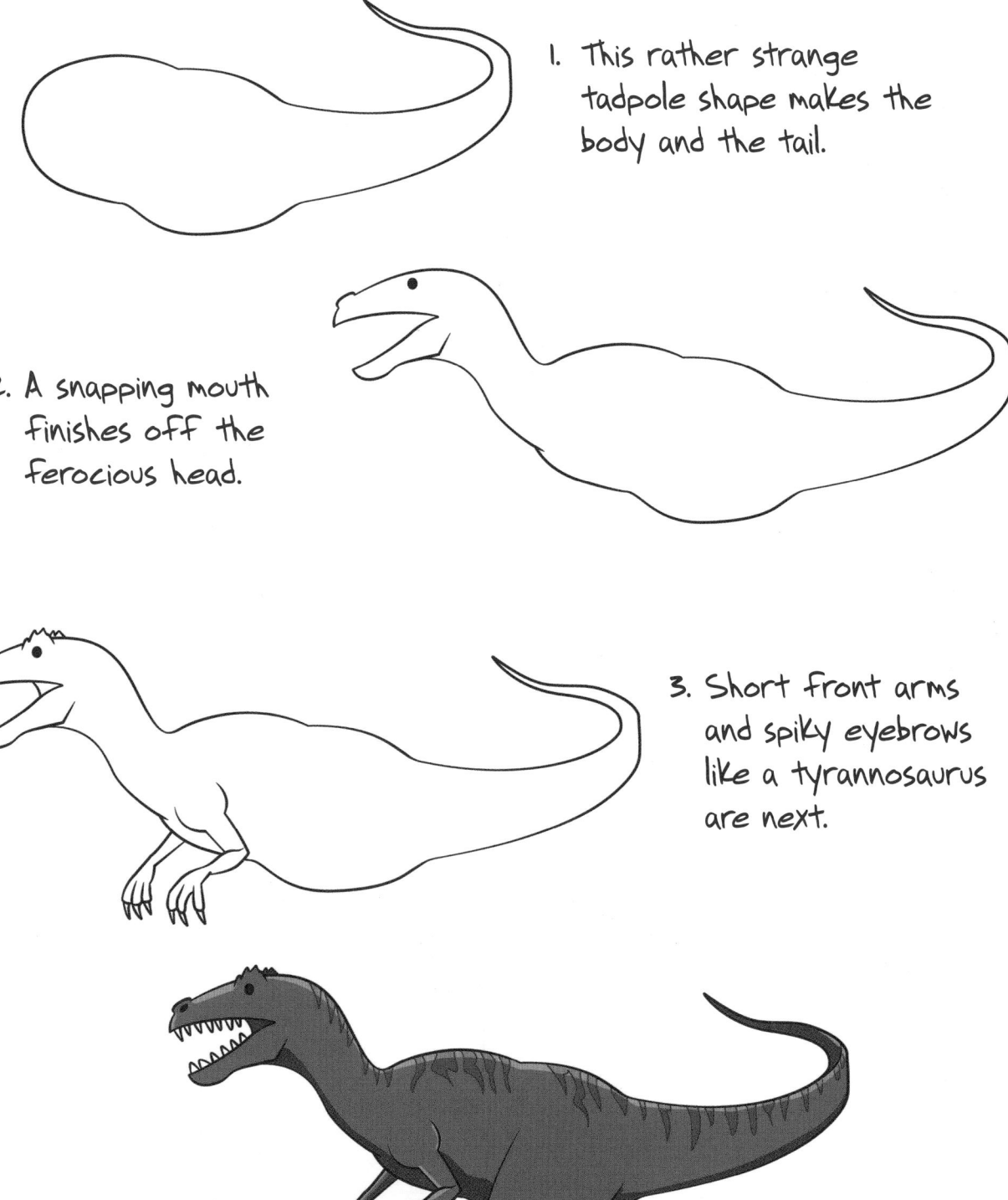

1. This rather strange tadpole shape makes the body and the tail.

2. A snapping mouth finishes off the ferocious head.

3. Short front arms and spiky eyebrows like a tyrannosaurus are next.

4. Muscular, powerful back legs finish off this frightening dino.

Brachiosaurus

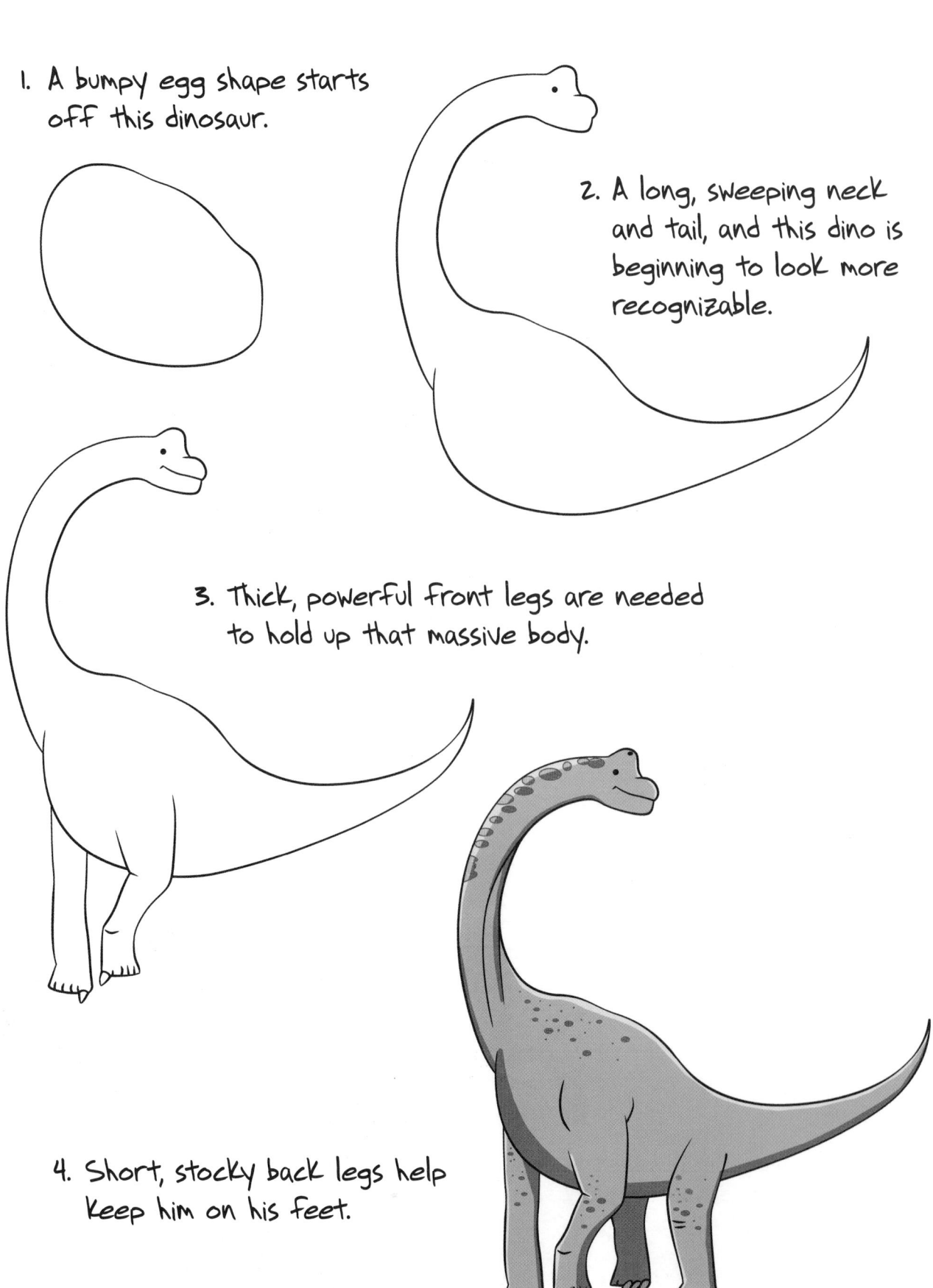

1. A bumpy egg shape starts off this dinosaur.

2. A long, sweeping neck and tail, and this dino is beginning to look more recognizable.

3. Thick, powerful front legs are needed to hold up that massive body.

4. Short, stocky back legs help keep him on his feet.

Oviraptor

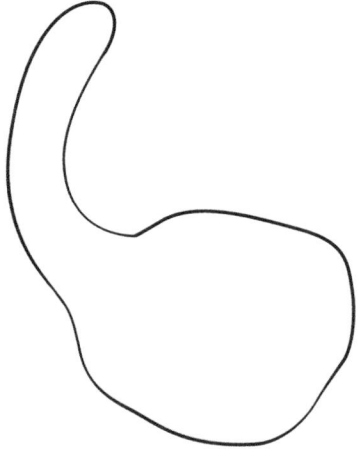

1. This dinosaur starts with a strange, fat tadpole shape.

2. A sharp, snapping beak and slashing tail make it look scary.

3. Muscular legs allow it to run at great speed.

4. Finish off the drawing with short, claw-tipped forelegs - not forgetting the feathery little wings!

Spinosaurus

1. Begin with this shape for the body.

2. Add a scary head with a long mouth and a powerful tail at the other end.

3. Draw a spiny sail on his back. Sharp, pointy teeth and claws are next.

4. Colour him in — but be careful you don't get gobbled up!

Megatherium

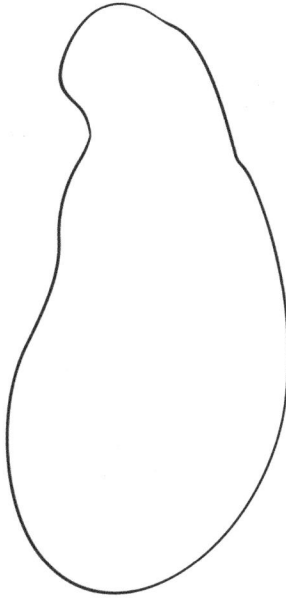

1. Start with a large squishy body.

2. Short chubby arms and a round chunky head are next.

3. Strong claws help him grab tree branches for food.

4. Remember to add plenty of thick fur when doing your final colouring.

Troodon

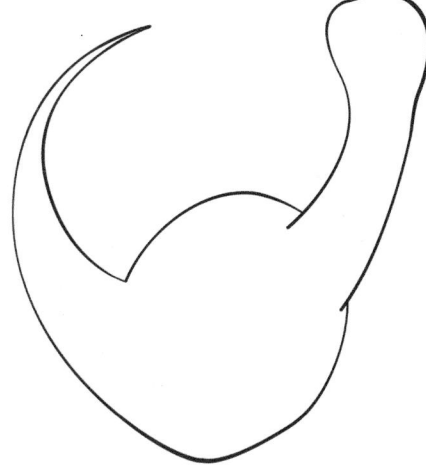

1. Draw the head, body and tail as one fluid shape.

2. Extend the nose and mouth and add sharp teeth.

3. This dinosaur has powerful legs and very sharp claws.

4. Add short front legs and don't forget the stripy back.

Megaloceros

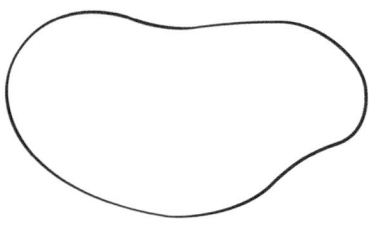

1. Draw the body shape.

2. Extend the neck and add a deer-shaped head.

3. The legs are just like a deer's, with dainty hooves.

4. Huge antlers set this creature apart from a modern-day stag.

Plesiosaurus

1. Draw an oval and add a tail shape to start with.

2. A long bendy neck and small head are next.

3. Large front and smaller back fins give added swimming power.

4. Choose either blue or brown for colouring.

Einiosaurus

1. Draw a fat tadpole shape for the body and tail.

2. A horned nose and bony plate behind the head give this dino extra protection.

3. Add powerful back legs, and two impressive horns on top of the head.

4. Stubby yet powerful front legs finish off this dinosaur.

Hesperosaurus

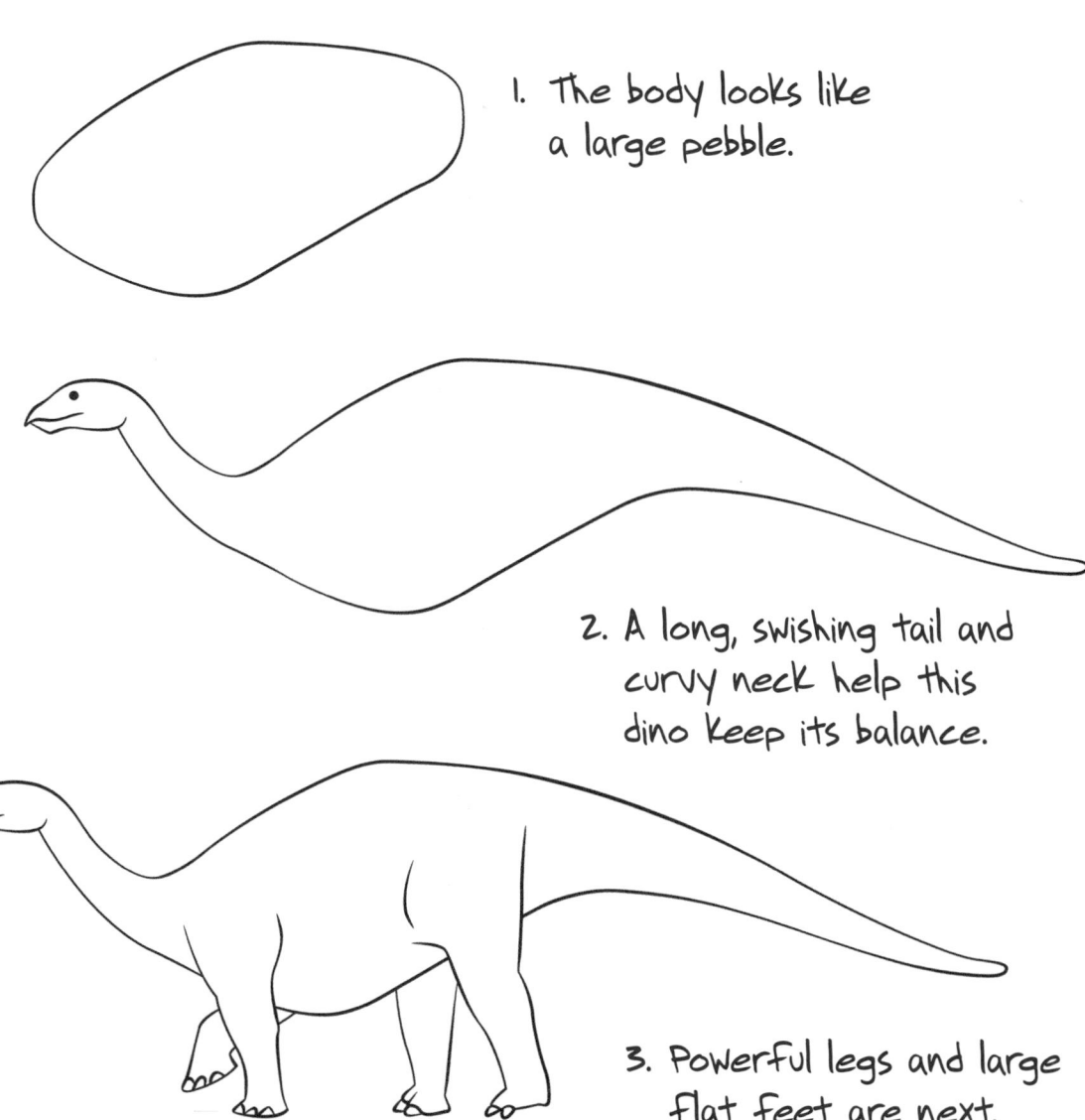

1. The body looks like a large pebble.

2. A long, swishing tail and curvy neck help this dino keep its balance.

3. Powerful legs and large flat feet are next.

4. An impressive collection of protective plates on its back adds the finishing touch.

Quetzalcoatlus

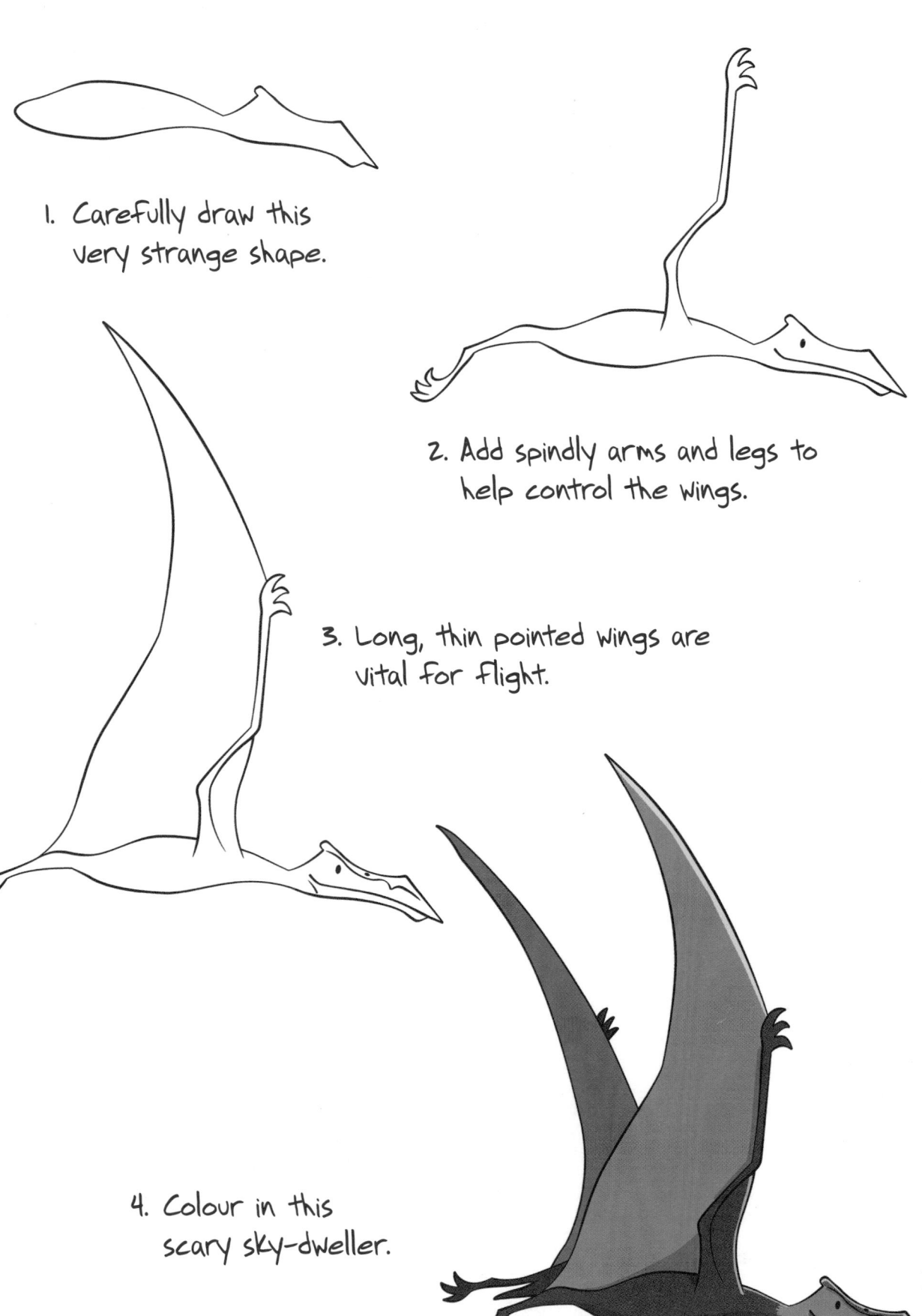

1. Carefully draw this very strange shape.

2. Add spindly arms and legs to help control the wings.

3. Long, thin pointed wings are vital for flight.

4. Colour in this scary sky-dweller.

Sabre-toothed Cat

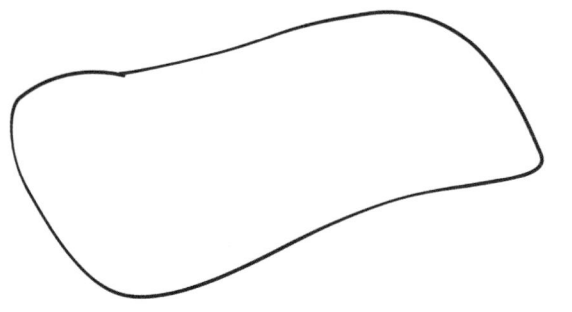

1. Draw this wobbly rectangle.

2. Add a long cat's tail and a fearsome head.

3. Huge, dagger-like teeth give him his name.

4. Add two more powerful legs and colour him in.

Jobs

Vet

1. Start with this shape for the head and body.

2. Add the hair and a cute little puppy.

3. Draw the legs and feet. Now you are ready to colour in the picture.

4. Don't forget to add the puppy's pink tongue.

Pilot

1. The strangely-shaped head includes the helmet too.

2. Add his trousers and gloves.

3. A flowing scarf and goggles are essential kit for a pilot.

4. Use shades of brown for the colour – and don't forget his moustache!

Fitness Instructor

1. Start by drawing a long, thin body and a round head.

2. Draw the arms and add the vest.

3. Draw some weights in her hands and a microphone on her head for giving directions.

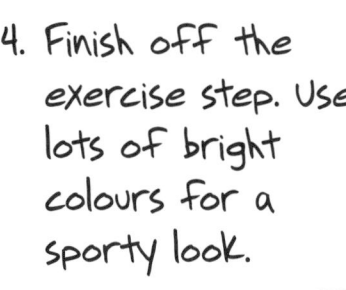

4. Finish off the exercise step. Use lots of bright colours for a sporty look.

Builder

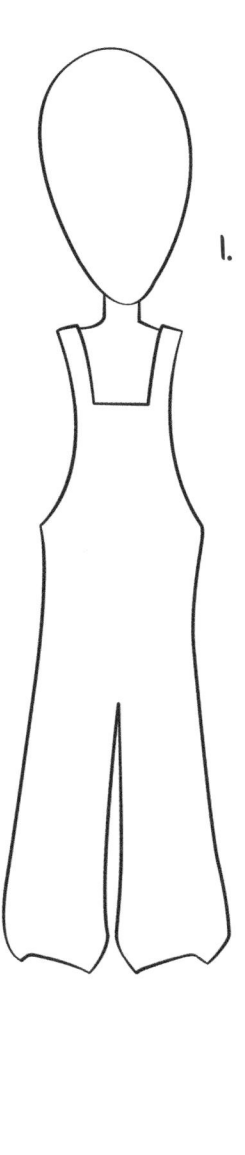

1. Start by drawing a pair of overalls and a head.

2. Add his arms and draw a line across the head to start the hard hat.

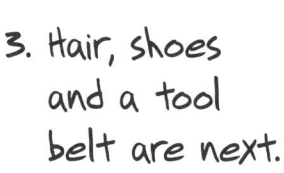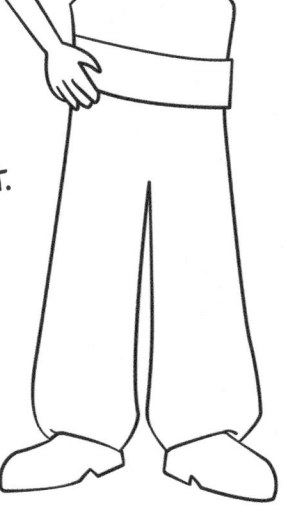

3. Hair, shoes and a tool belt are next.

4. Add tools to the belt. Finish off by colouring the builder in.

Secret Agent

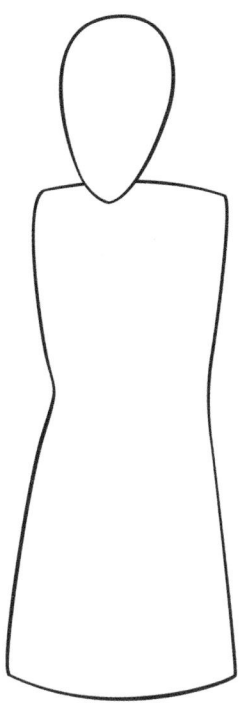

1. Begin with this shape for the body.

2. Add the hat, arms, and a magnifying glass.

3. Give him a trench coat, like a real spy.

4. Colour him in browns and greys so that he can blend in with his surroundings.

Teacher

1. Draw the face and upper body to start with. Have one arm raised, as though she is pointing.

2. Make the teacher look smart, with a jacket and skirt.

3. Give her a book in one hand and a pointer in the other.

4. Colour her in. Include a blackboard, so the teacher looks as though she's in a classroom.

Cabin-crew Member

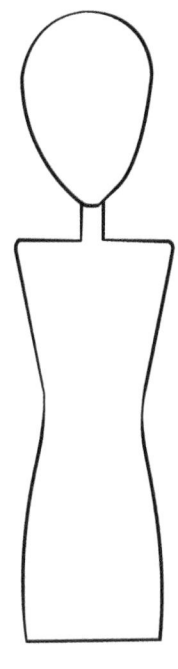

1. Start with an hourglass shape for the body.

2. Divide the shape with a line to create the skirt and then draw in a hat and handbag.

3. Add legs, hair and a scarf.

4. Finish the picture with some cheerful colours. Keep her hair tidy with a hairnet.

Trapeze Artist

1. Draw a jellybean shape for the body and a squashed oval for the head.

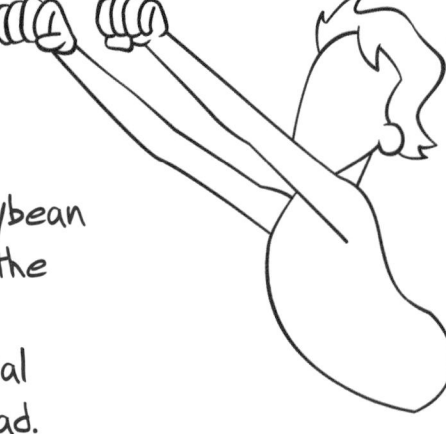

2. Add outstretched arms. Make the hair look as though it is being blown by the wind.

3. The curve of the body, and legs flung back make it look as though he is swinging.

4. Give him a trapeze to hold on to, then finish with lots of bright colours.

Racing Driver

1. The racing suit makes up most of this body shape.

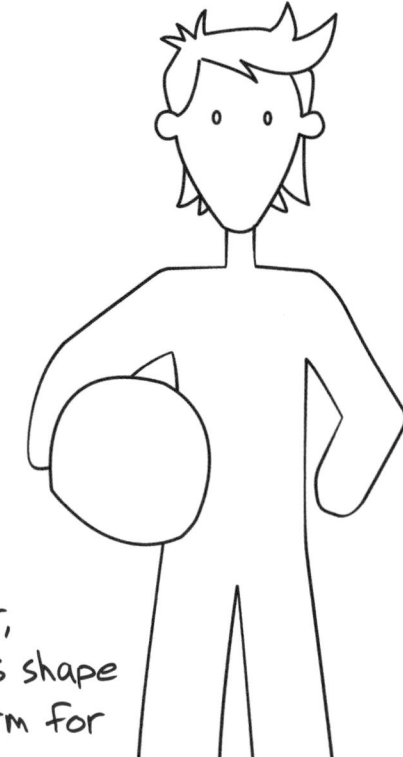

2. Give him hair, then add this shape under the arm for his helmet.

3. Add a visor and give the driver some hands and feet.

4. Colour him in, being sure to give him some bright racing colours on his suit.

Sailor

1. This very odd shape for the head also includes the sailor's hat.

2. Add some hands and a simple line to divide the head and the hat.

3. Make him look more like a sailor by adding bell-bottomed trousers and a ship's rope.

4. Make him lean back a little to show that he is pulling on the rope.

Jockey

1. Start wioth a basic horse body shape.

2. Draw the upper half of the jockey. Show the horse's mane flowing backwards to make it look as though the horse is running.

3. Complete the jockey and the horse's legs.

4. Colour in your picture, not forgetting to add a saddle and bridle.

Chef

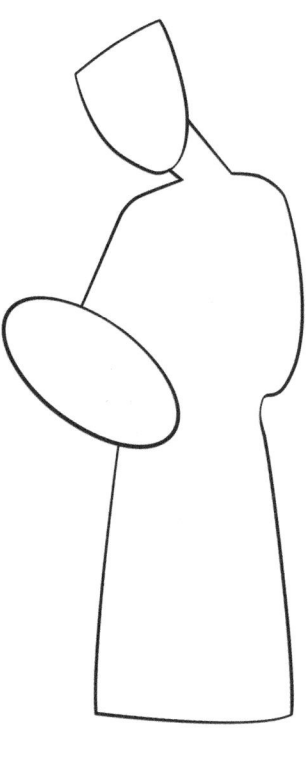

1. Copy this shape to make the head, body and start of the mixing bowl.

2. Complete the bowl and add the chef's hat.

3. Give her some legs and add an apron and a wooden spoon.

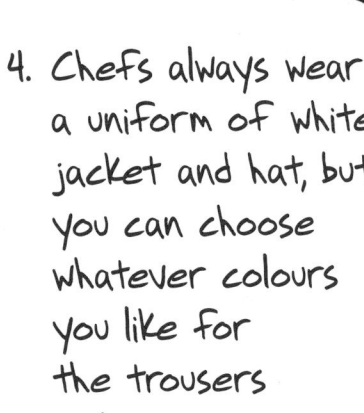

4. Chefs always wear a uniform of white jacket and hat, but you can choose whatever colours you like for the trousers and apron.

Singer

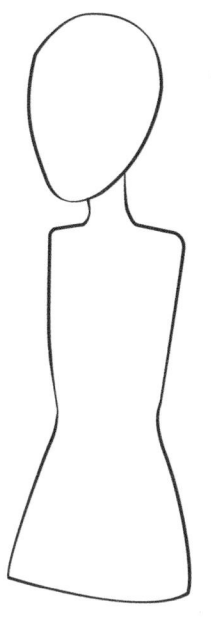

1. Draw this curvy shape for the body.

2. Add the arms and long, flowing hair.

3. A funky dress and the all-important microphone are next.

4. Colour her in. Use bright, fun colours for her clothes.

TV Cameraman

1. Draw the head and the body.

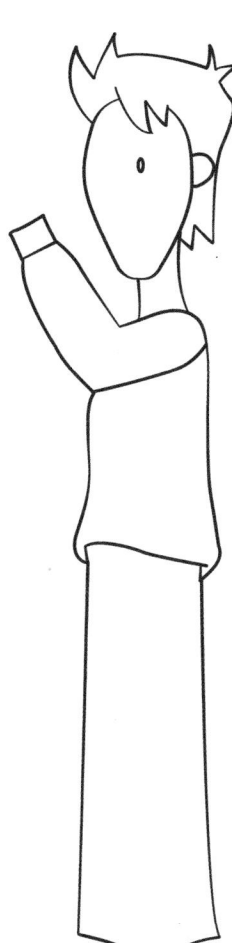

2. Add trousers and hair.

3. Simple shapes make up the camera.

4. Colouring the lens blue will make it look like glass.

Judge

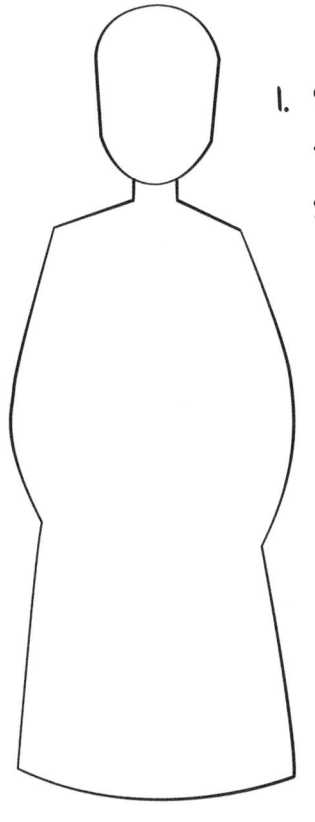

1. Start with these simple shapes.

2. Add a judge's wig and give him some arms.

3. A cloak and moustache make him look important.

4. Judges' robes are a very deep red colour.

Lifeguard

1. This shape makes up the top half of the body.

2. Add her hair, shorts and a life-saving float.

3. Draw detail on the hands and add a sash that connects to the float. Pencil in the legs.

4. Make sure you colour the float bright orange so it can be seen during rescues.

Astronaut

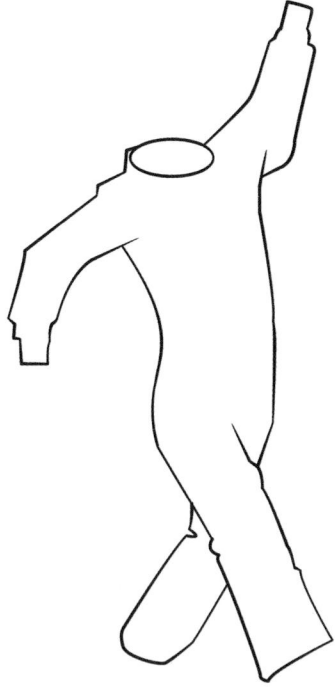

1. This shape will give you the whole body in one go.

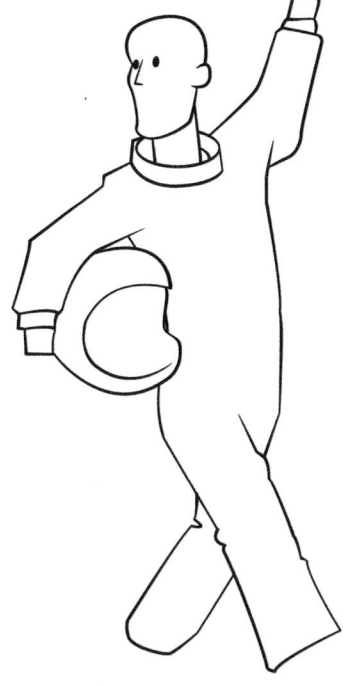

2. Add the astronaut's head, and a helmet under his arm.

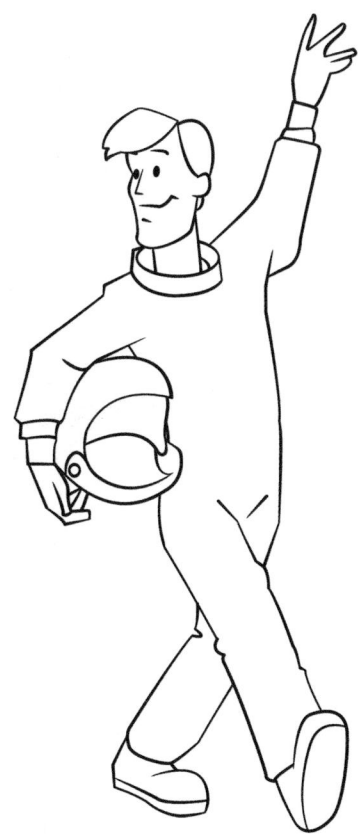

3. Hair, boots and hands are next.

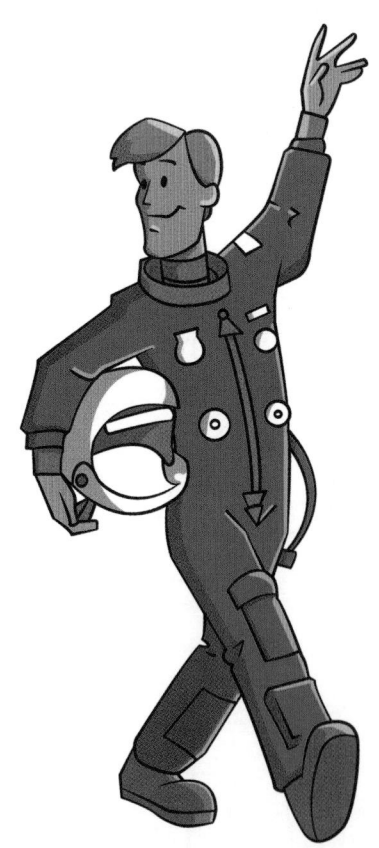

4. Colour the astronaut's flight suit orange.

Creepy Crawlies

Scorpion

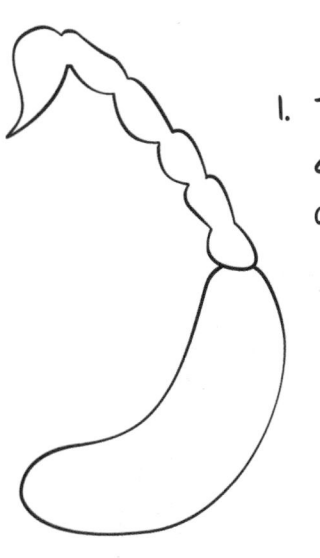

1. This weird shape is a clue to what you are drawing.

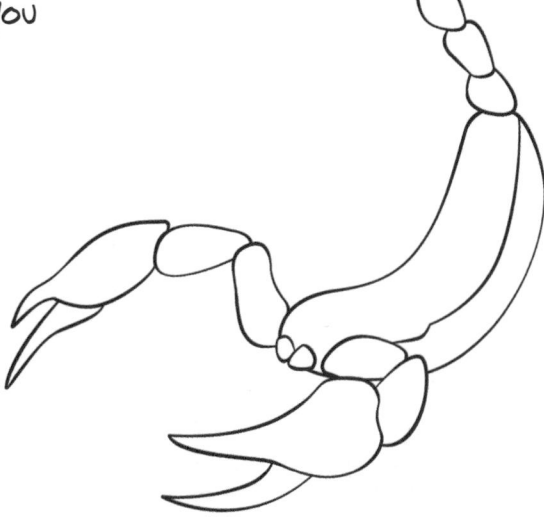

2. Add snapping pincers at the front.

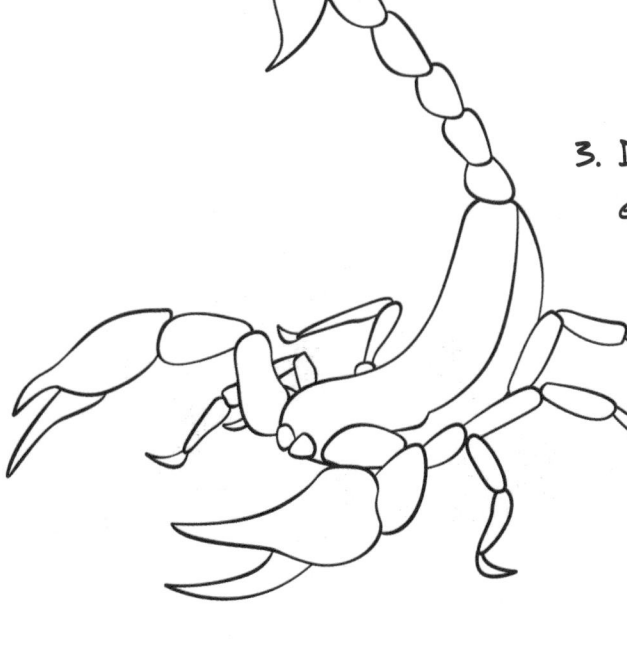

3. Don't forget three legs on either side of the body.

4. Colour in your creation, but mind you don't get stung by that tail!

Praying Mantis

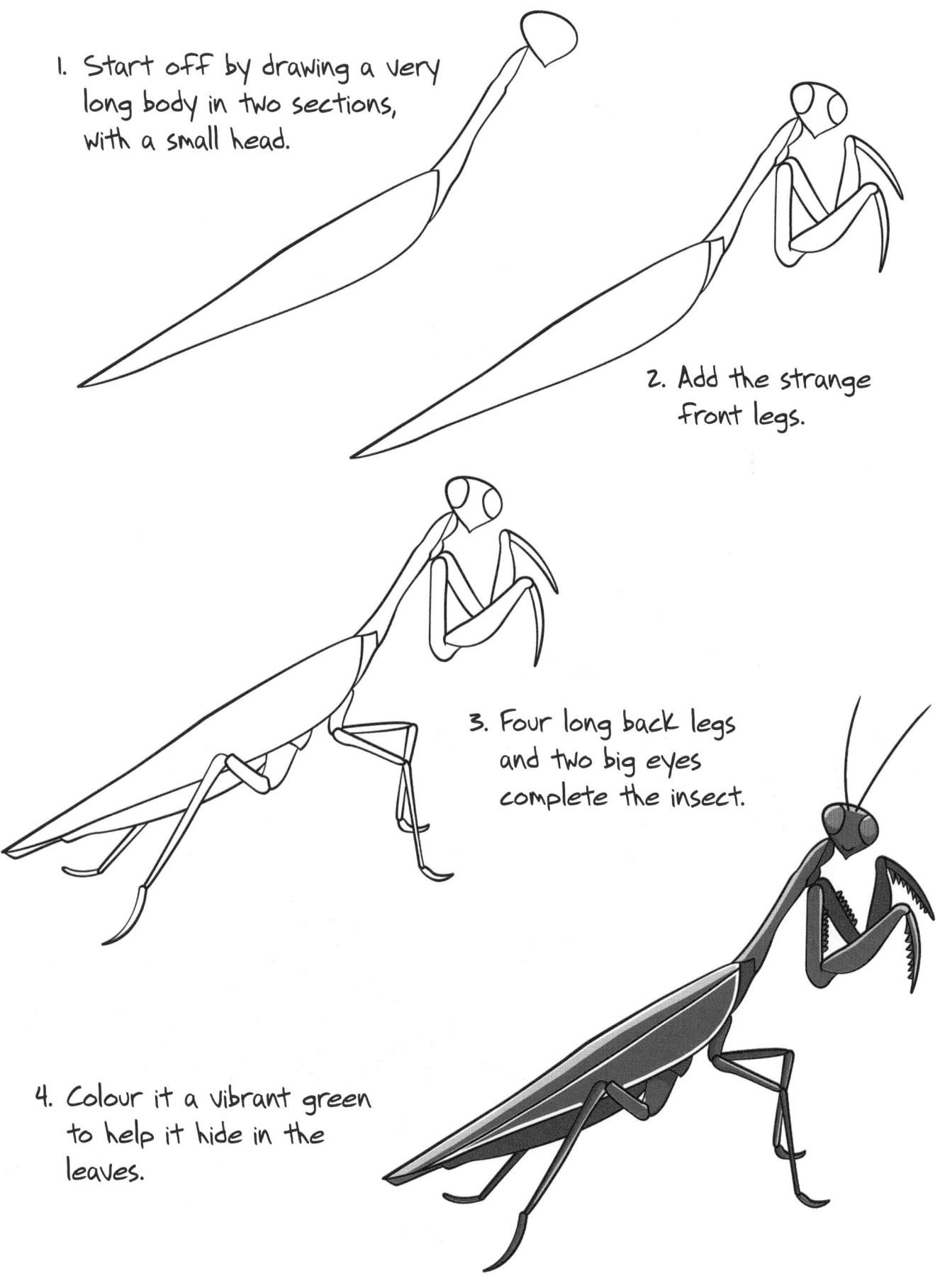

1. Start off by drawing a very long body in two sections, with a small head.

2. Add the strange front legs.

3. Four long back legs and two big eyes complete the insect.

4. Colour it a vibrant green to help it hide in the leaves.

Fly

1. Start with this shape.

2. Add the large wings.

3. Thin but powerful legs are next.

4. Colour it in, making the
   wings light blue for a
   see-through effect.
   Don't forget to add
   spiky hairs on the body.

Caterpillar

1. An extra-long sausage shape makes the body.

2. Draw lots of little legs along the the bottom of the body.

3. Add plenty of stripes to make it stand out.

4. Lots of bright colours and big antennae finish off this happy caterpillar.

Snail

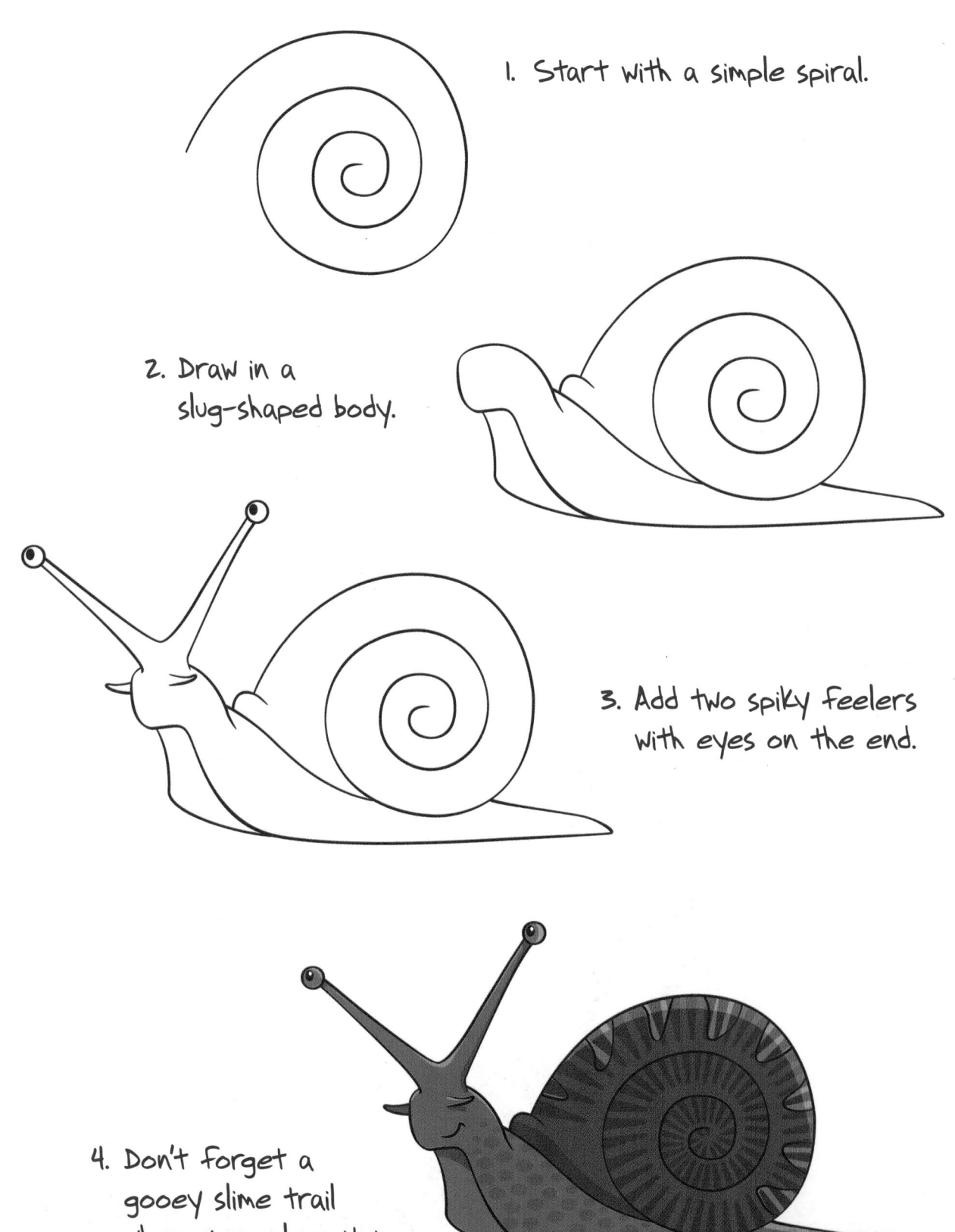

1. Start with a simple spiral.

2. Draw in a slug-shaped body.

3. Add two spiky feelers with eyes on the end.

4. Don't forget a gooey slime trail when you colour it in.

Ladybird

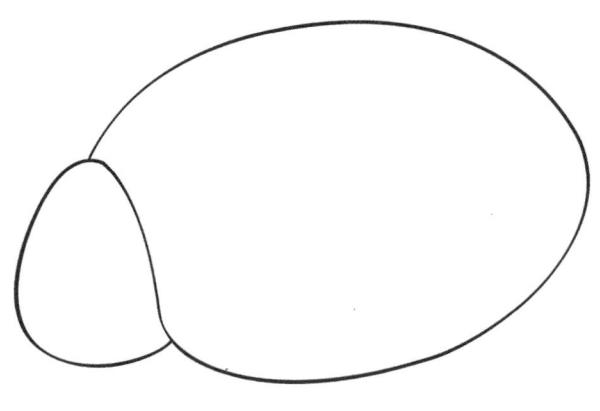

1. Draw two circles, one big and one small, for the body and head.

2. Divide the head and body with simple lines.

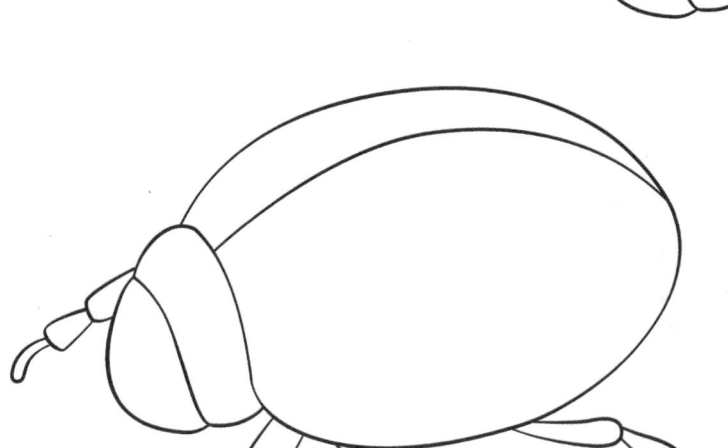

3. Add some short legs. The ladybird has six legs, but you can only see four in this picture.

4. Colour your ladybird bright red with black spots.

Butterfly

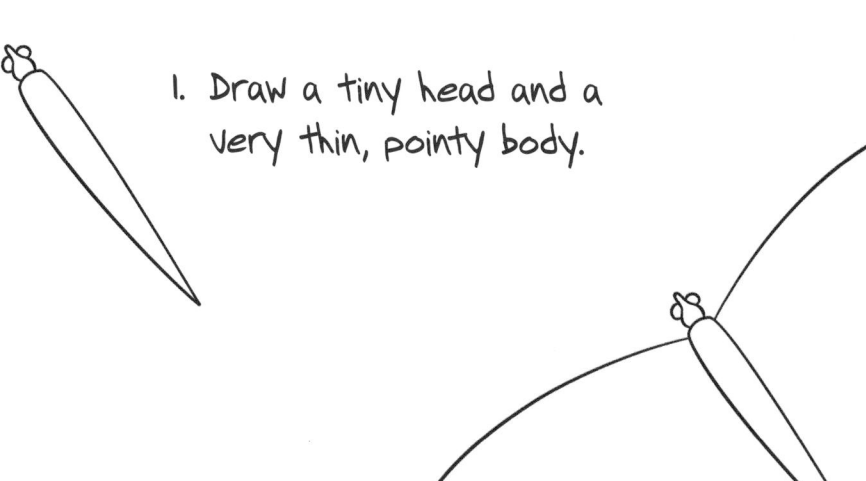

1. Draw a tiny head and a very thin, pointy body.

2. Huge, flat wings help it to fly.

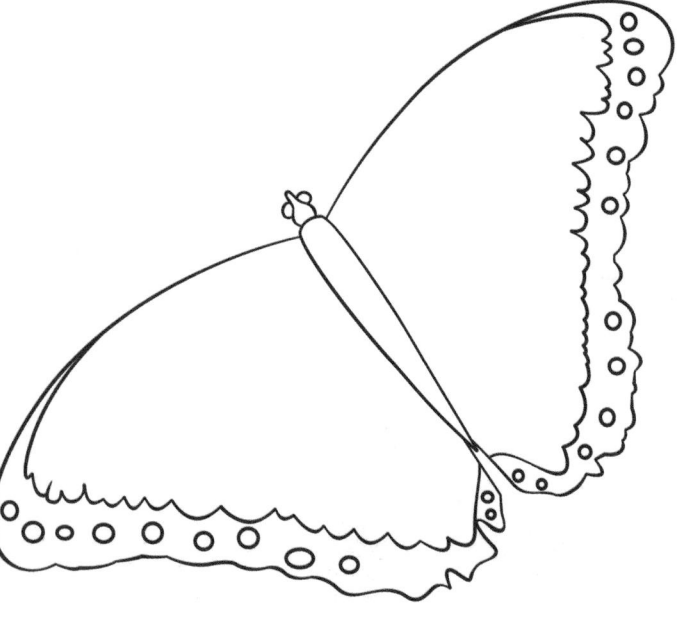

3. Add some patterning around the edges of the wings.

4. Colour your butterfly a pretty bright blue. Give the wings a black border with white spots.

Grasshopper

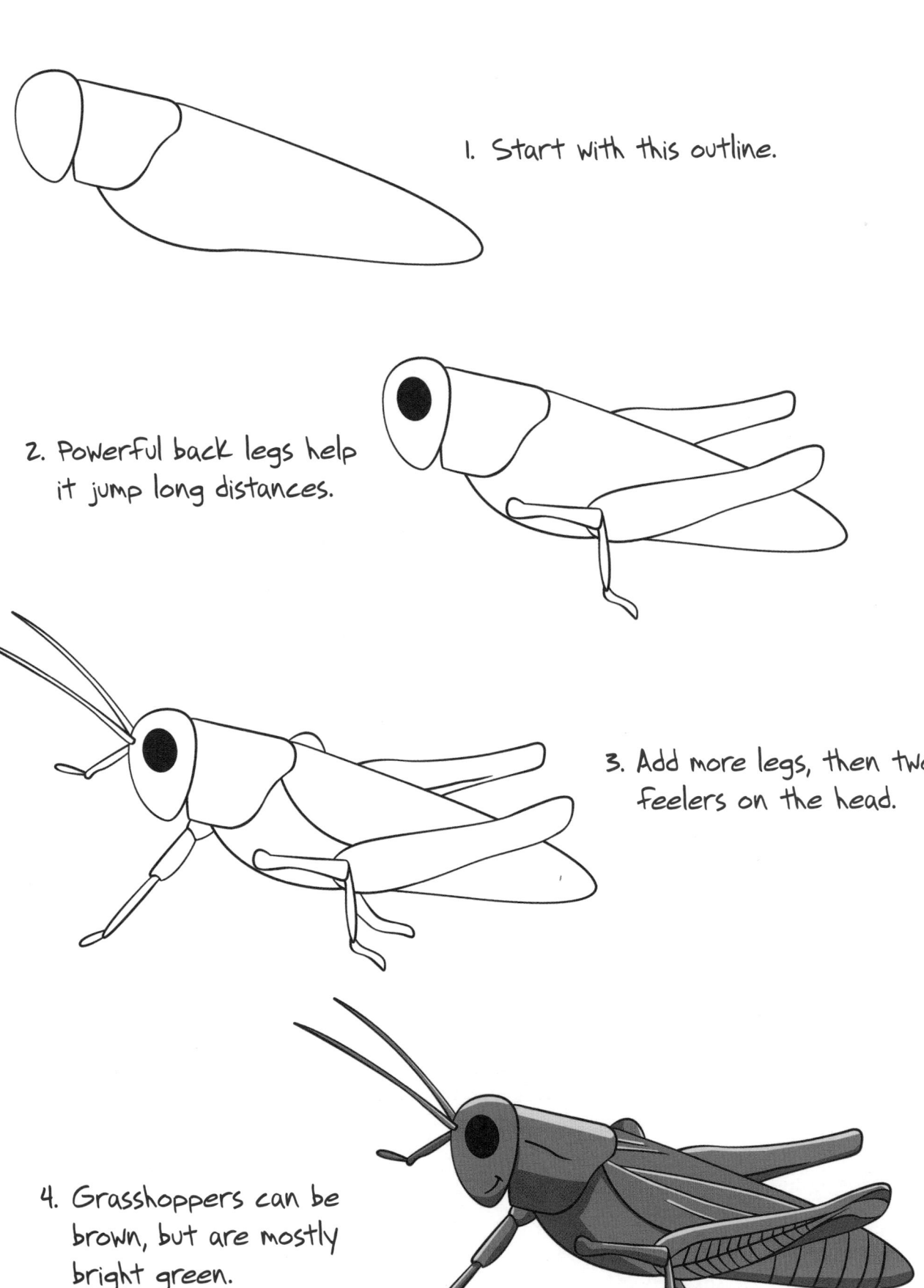

1. Start with this outline.

2. Powerful back legs help it jump long distances.

3. Add more legs, then two feelers on the head.

4. Grasshoppers can be brown, but are mostly bright green.

Dragonfly

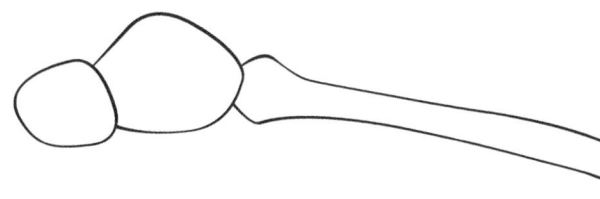

1. Draw this strange collection of shapes to make the head and body.

2. Add some spindly legs. Dragonflies have six legs, but you can only see four in this picture.

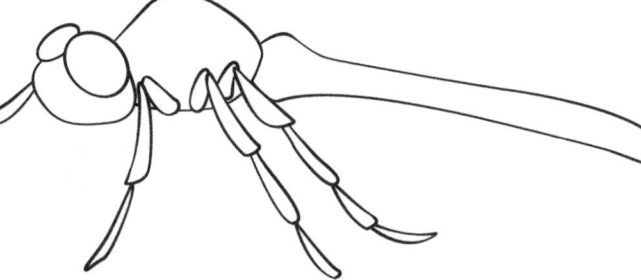

3. Draw four long, narrow wings. These enable the insect to hover.

4. Colour the wings pale blue to make them seem see-through.

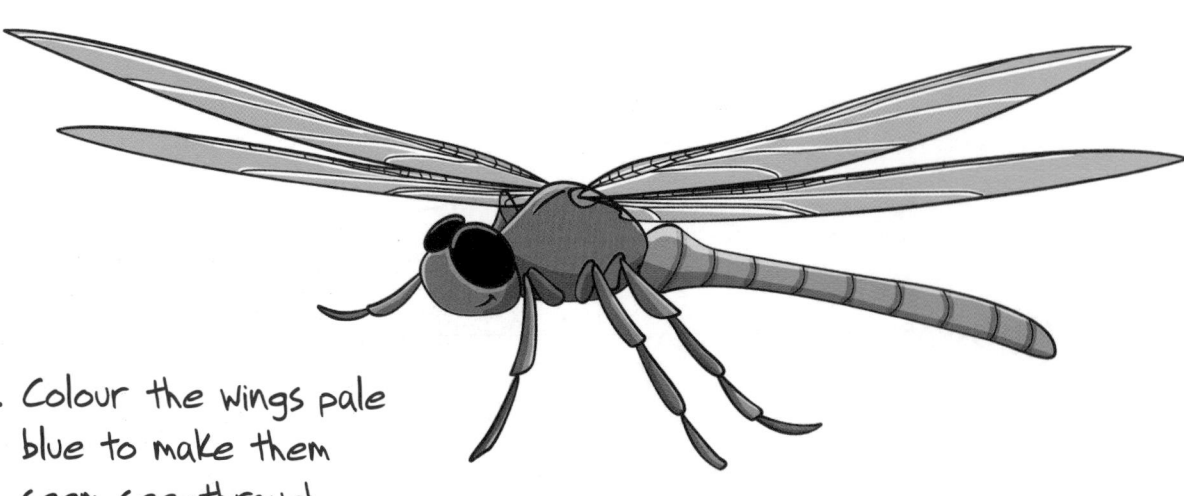

Centipede

1. Draw a long, curvy sausage shape with a circle at the top.

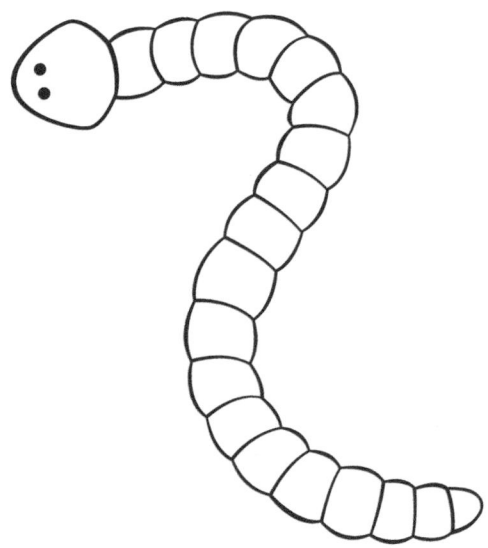

2. Now draw in the segments of the body.

3. Add lots and lots of legs!

4. Colour him in – don't forget the feelers on his head.

Stag Beetle

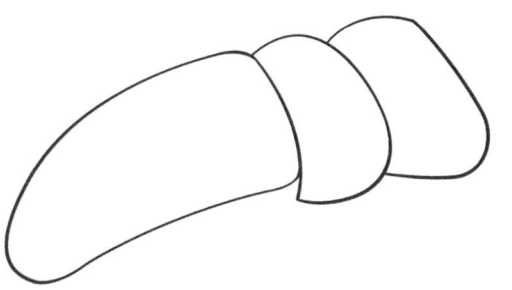

1. Two squashed circles and one long oval make the head and body.

2. Add two fierce pincers at the front.

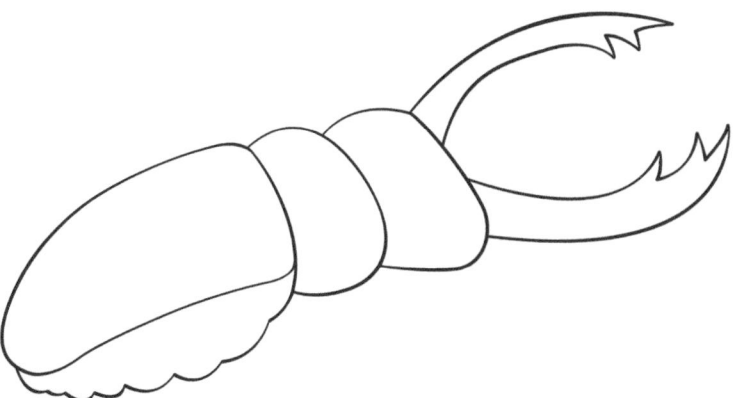

3. Draw spindly legs that get thinner at the end.

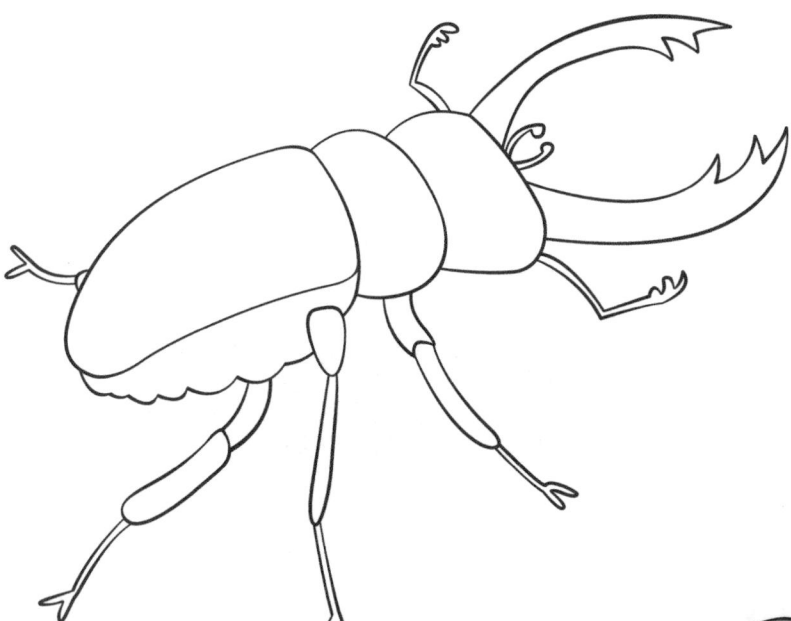

4. Brown and black are the colours you'll need to finish it off.

Millipede

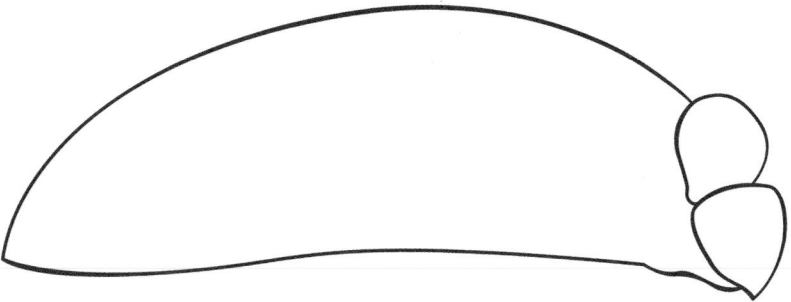

1. Draw a long, fat sausage with two small teardrop shapes at one end.

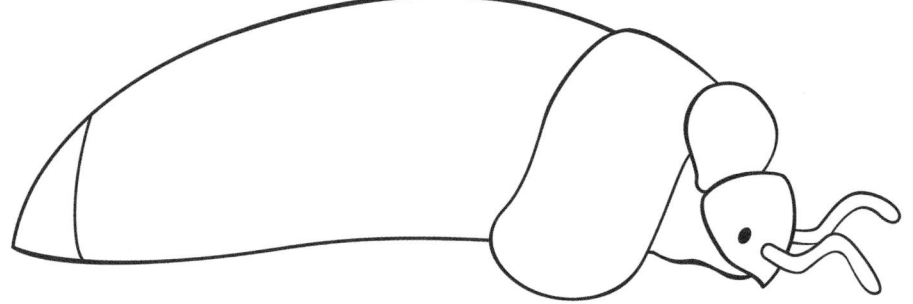

2. Add the first body segment, eye and feelers.

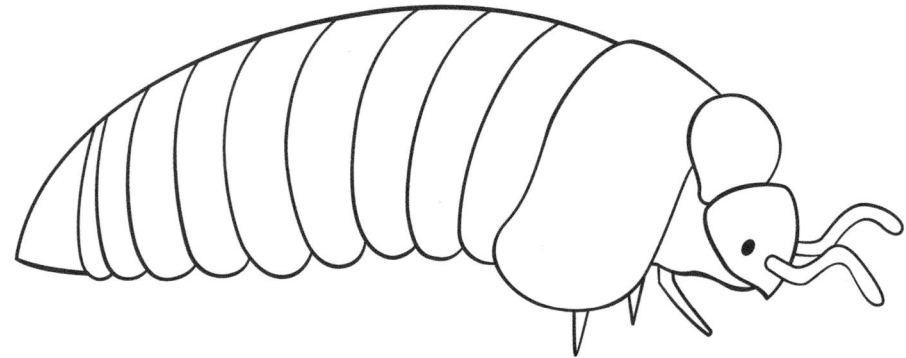

3. Draw in the rest of the eleven body segments and start adding the legs.

4. Finish adding the legs, colour it in, and you are done.

Moth

1. Draw a first shape similar to that of the butterfly, but with a much thicker body.

2. Add two large, flat upper wings.

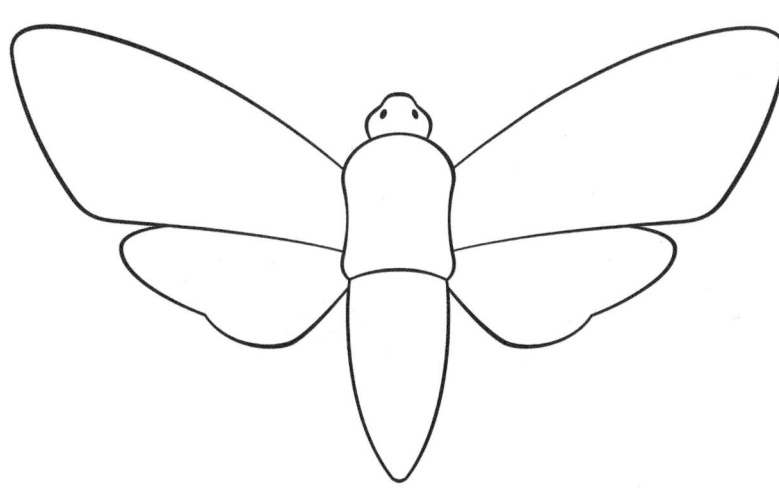

3. Add two smaller lower wings. These help the insect to steer in flight.

4. Colour it in and add a stripy body, if you like.

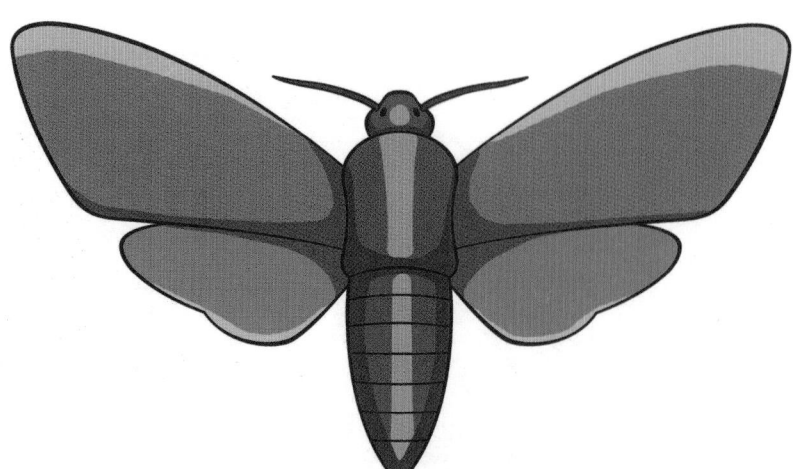

Ant

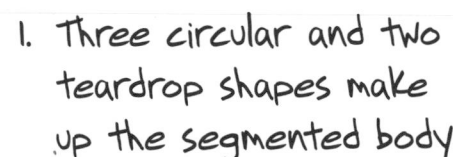

1. Three circular and two teardrop shapes make up the segmented body.

2. Add two eyes to the head and six spindly legs to the body.

3. Finish the legs with points, and you are nearly done.

4. Colour it in. Ants can be black, brown or even red.

Bumblebee

1. A fluffy body and head start it off.

2. The little wings fold flat against its body when not in use.

3. Add three legs on either side of the body.

4. Black and yellow are the colours for a bee. Use pale blue to make the wings look thin and light.

On the Beach

Crab

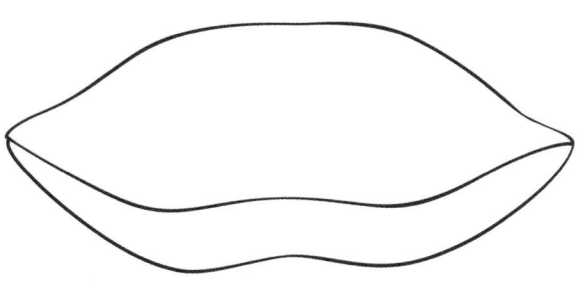

1. Draw a shape that looks like a pair of lips.

2. Add some eyes and two big snapping claws.

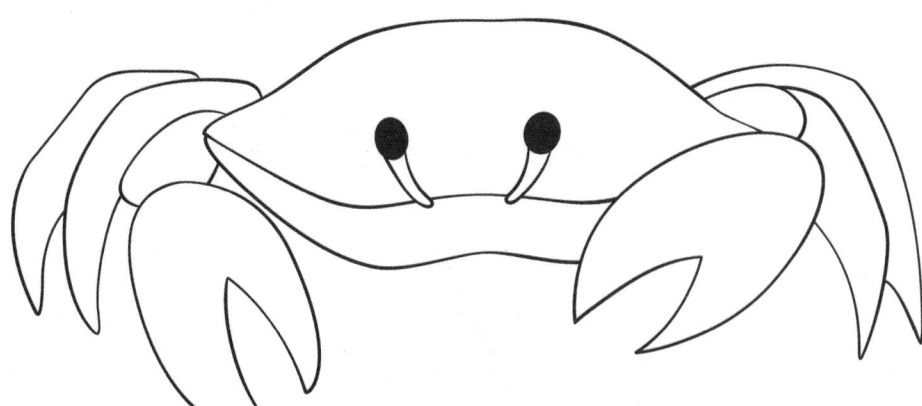

3. Draw the back legs. Crabs have ten legs, but you can only see six in this picture.

4. Use a rich orange-brown colour to finish off your picture.

Surfer

1. Draw the head and a long body.

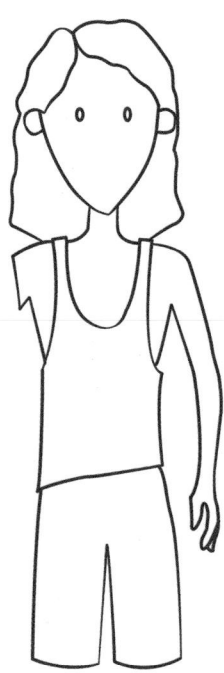

2. Divide the body into a vest and shorts, then add his hair.

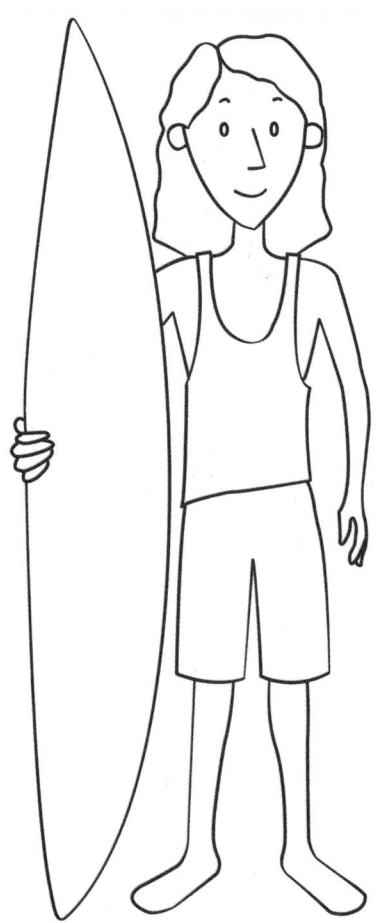

3. Add the surfboard - don't forget to draw his fingers holding it.

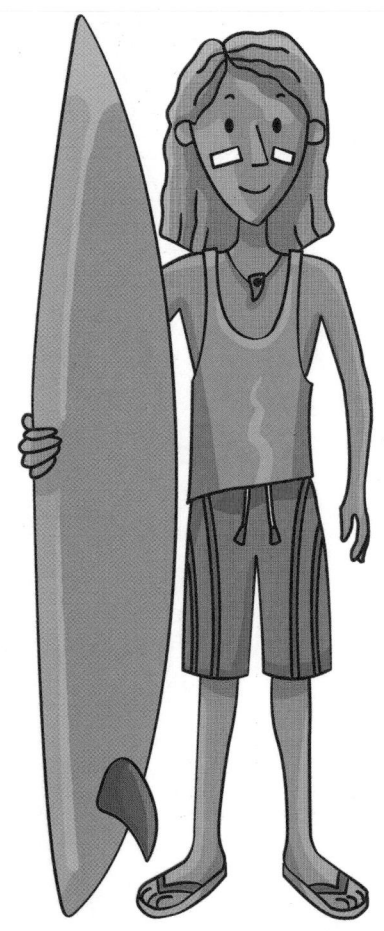

4. Add flip-flops and lots of bright colours to create a summery look.

Snorkeller

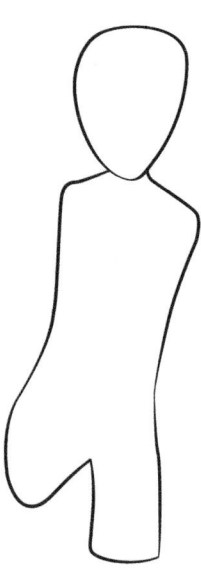

1. Start with this shape.

2. Add arms and give him some sticking-up hair.

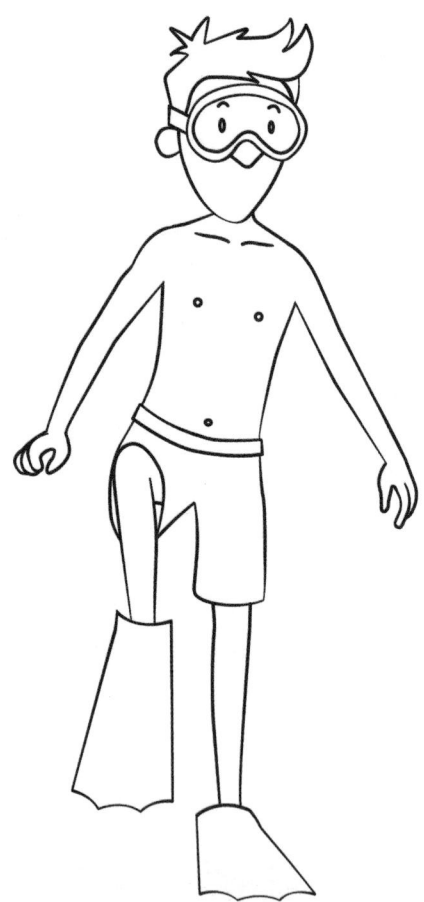

3. Draw two legs with flippers on the feet and add his snorkelling mask.

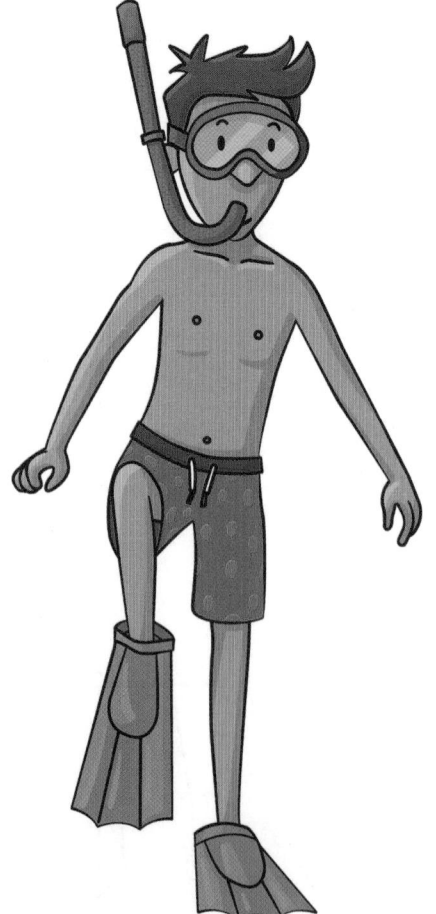

4. Finish off by adding a snorkel, then colour him in.

Seashells

1. Start by drawing the starfish.

2. Add some rough shell shapes.

3. Draw curved lines as detail on the shells.

4. The starfish needs to be orange, but the shells can be any colour you like.

Sunbather

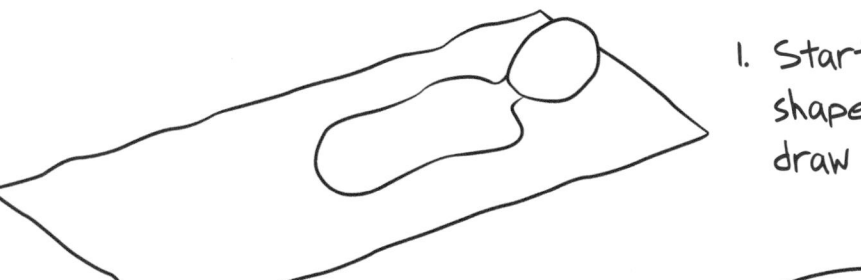

1. Start with a rectangular shape for the towel, then draw the head and body.

2. Add hair and sunglasses and a half-sphere for the umbrella.

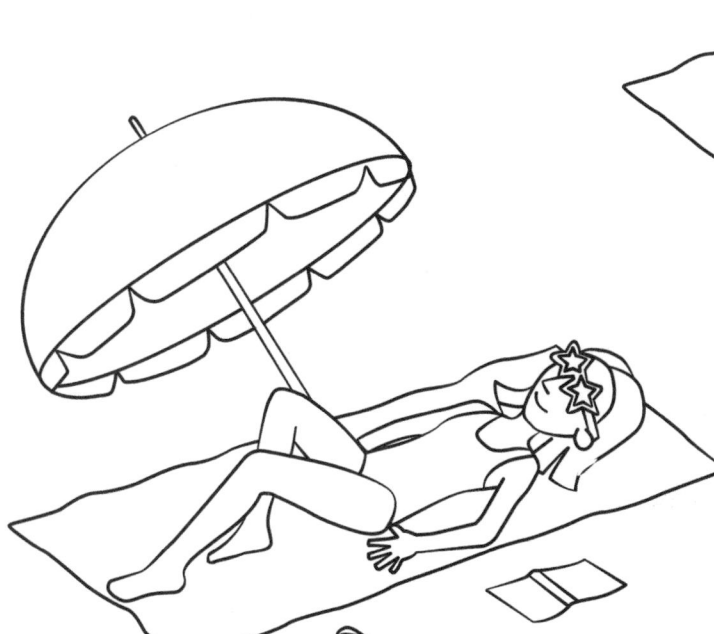

3. Next add legs and finish the arms and the umbrella.

4. Colour in the picture, using bright shades for the umbrella and towel. Add a sandy beach for the sunbather to lie on.

Kite-Flyer

1. Begin by drawing this shape.

2. The kite-flyer is wearing shorts and the wind is blowing his hair.

3. Outstretched arms and legs show he's running to pull the kite along.

4. Add some bows to the kite's tail, and colour the picture brightly.

Rowing Boat

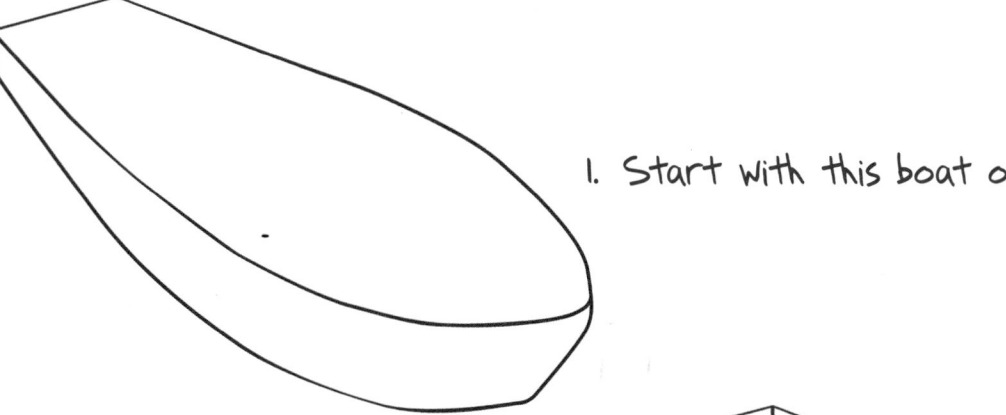

1. Start with this boat outline.

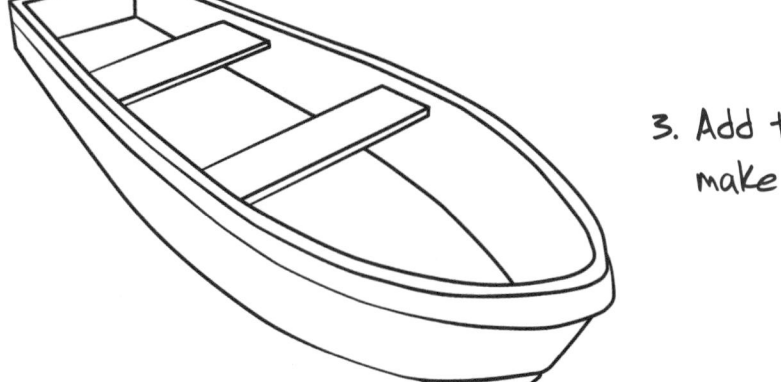

2. Add lines like this to make the inside of the boat.

3. Add two rectangles to make the seats.

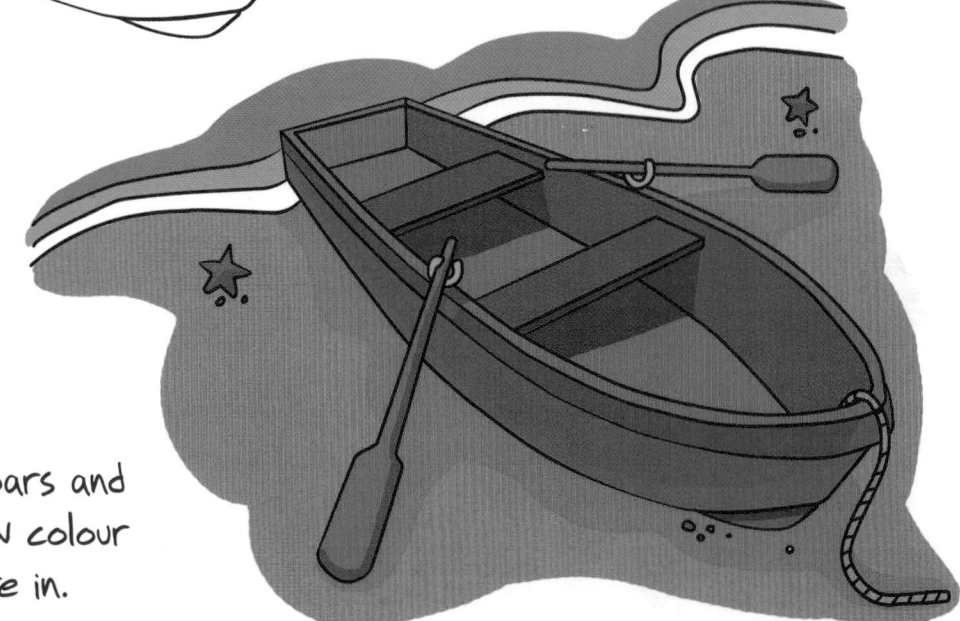

4. Draw two oars and a rope. Now colour your picture in.

Bucket and Spade

1. Start by drawing the bucket and the end of the spade.

2. Add the handle of the spade and the lip of the bucket.

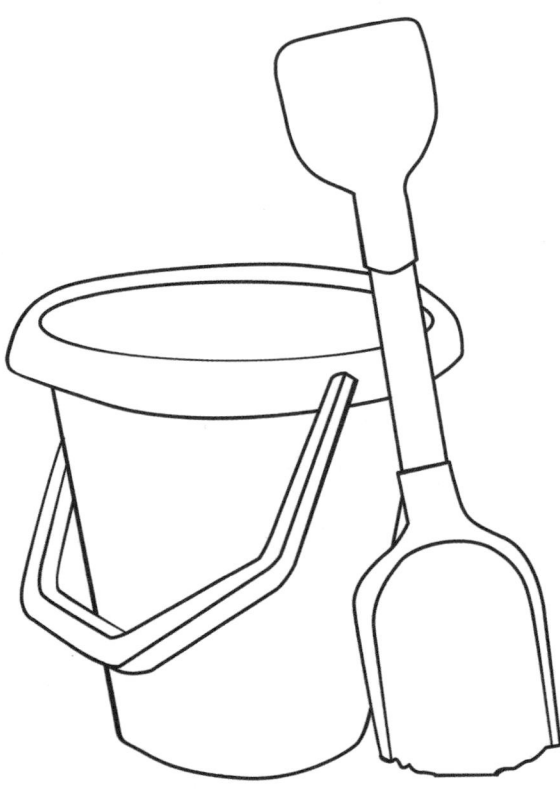

3. Draw the bucket handle and the inside of the spade.

4. Add sand inside the bucket and colour your picture in.

Girl with Beach Ball

1. Draw the head and body.

2. Add her arms, hair and a beach ball.

3. Add her legs and give her a ponytail.

4. Make the ball look as though it's moving by drawing lines between it and the girl.

Ice Cream

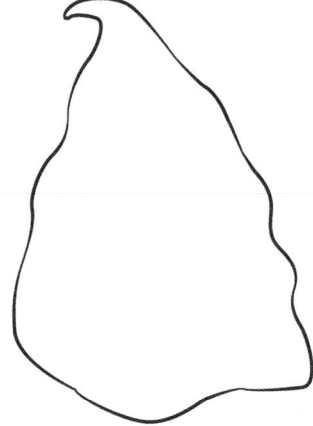

1. Start with this wobbly shape.

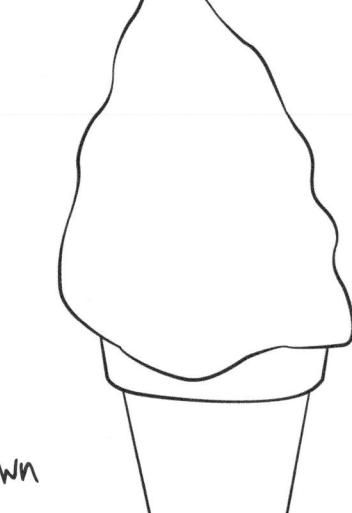

2. Draw an upside-down triangle for the cone.

3. Add a rectangle for the flake.

4. Colour the cone in two different shades of light brown.

Sea Kayaker

1. Begin with this shape.

2. Draw in the arms and hair, and give her a life jacket.

3. Add a long pole for the main paddle.

4. Draw the blades at the ends of the pole and colour the picture in.

Beach Girl

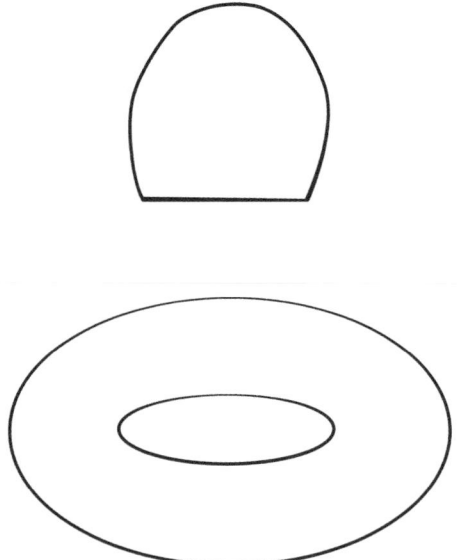
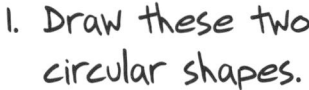

1. Draw these two circular shapes.

2. Add the top half of the body, hair, sunglasses, and a duck's-head feature on the rubber ring.

3. Add the girl's legs, and you are almost done.

4. Finish off with a flower hairclip and a pair of flip-flops, and colour her in.

Lighthouse

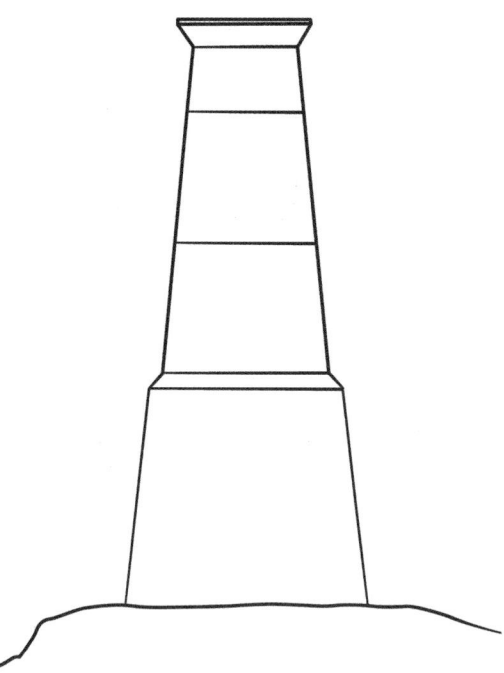

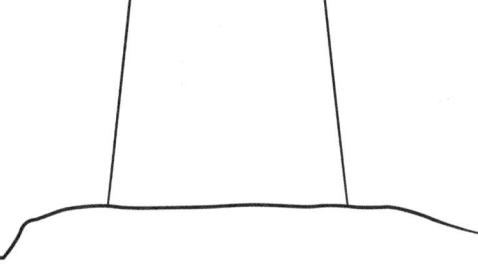

1. Draw this block shape and add a line underneath for the rock.

2. Add more blocks on top.

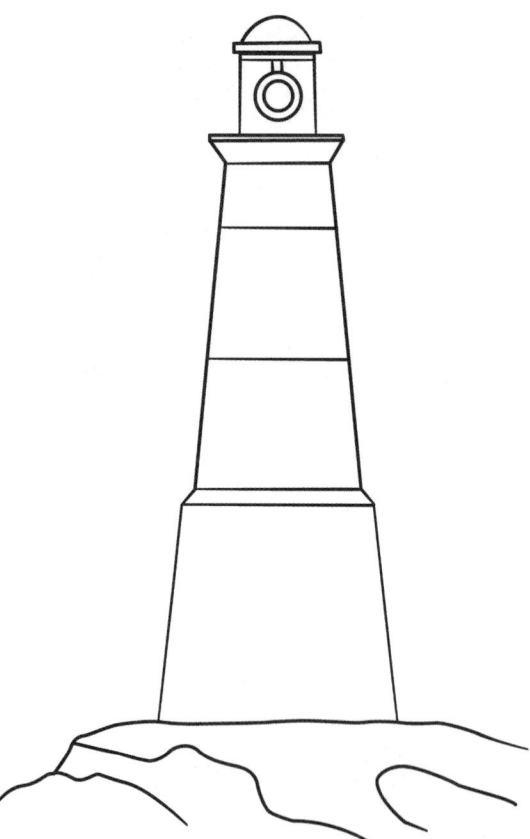

3. Draw the top level and the light itself.

4. Colour your lighthouse red and white so ships can see it easily.

Pedalo

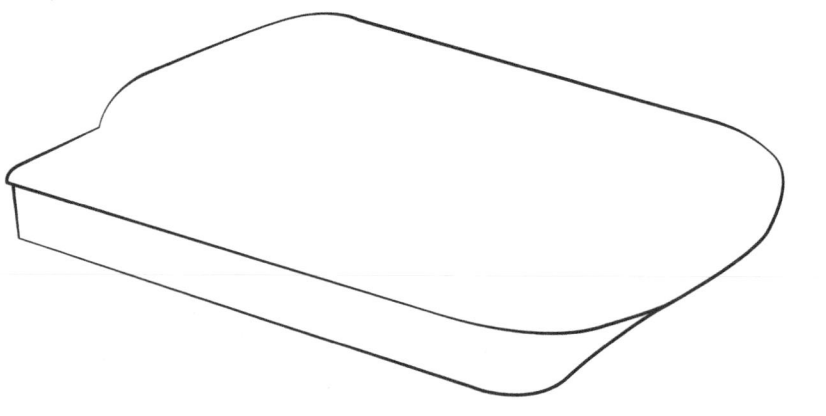

1. Start with this strange shape.

2. Add these lines to create the inside of the pedalo.

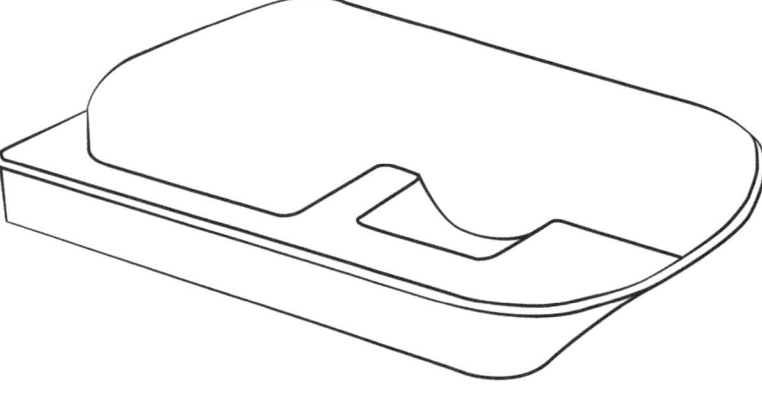

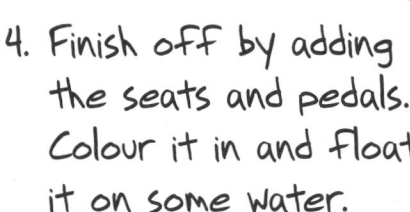

3. Draw the curved piece in the middle to house the paddles.

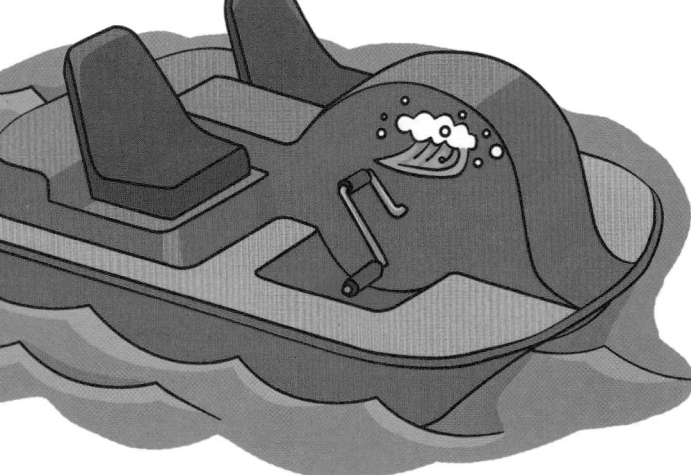

4. Finish off by adding the seats and pedals. Colour it in and float it on some water.

Tropical Island

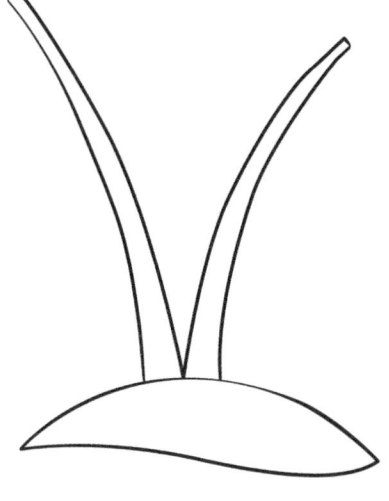

1. A mound and two bending trunks are your starting point.

2. Divide the trunks into segments and add leaves at the top.

3. Draw little V shapes along the edges of the leaves.

4. Give the picture some tropical colours. Don't forget to add some water round the island.

Sandcastle

1. Start with these curved rectangles. The front pair look like upside-down chimney pots.

2. Add defensive walls round the top of the towers. Add spires to two of them.

3. Draw walls to link the towers together.

4. Colour your castle in a bright, sandy yellow.

Beach Buggy

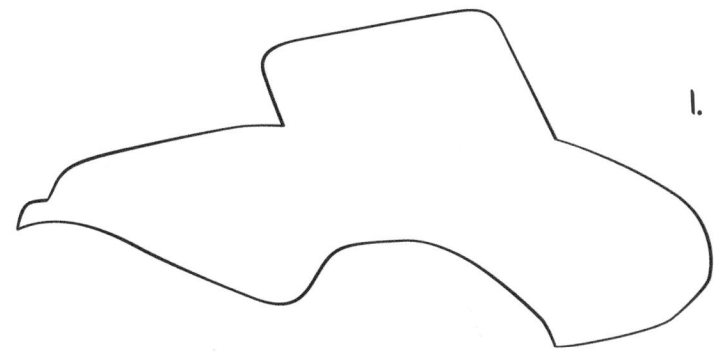

1. Draw this curvy shape for the body.

2. Add the wheels, mudguards and windscreen.

3. Draw some seats and a rollbar at the front.

4. Colour the windscreen blue to make it look like glass.

Pets

Gerbil

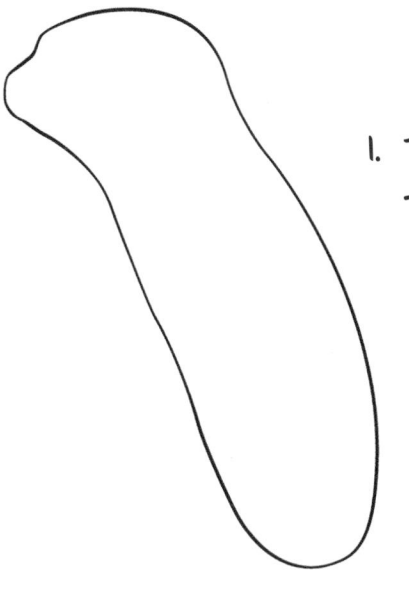

1. This shape gives you the body and head.

2. Add the ears, nose, mouth and eyes.

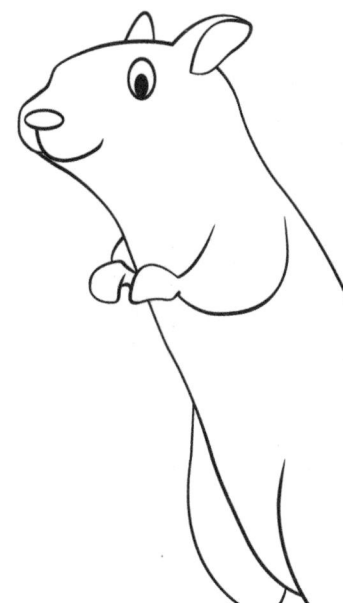

3. Short, stubby front legs and larger more powerful back legs are next.

4. Don't forget to add the tail. This looks like a mouse's tail with a furry bit at the end. Colour in the brown body and the little pink hands and feet.

Tarantula

1. Start with two furry circles and a pair of fangs.

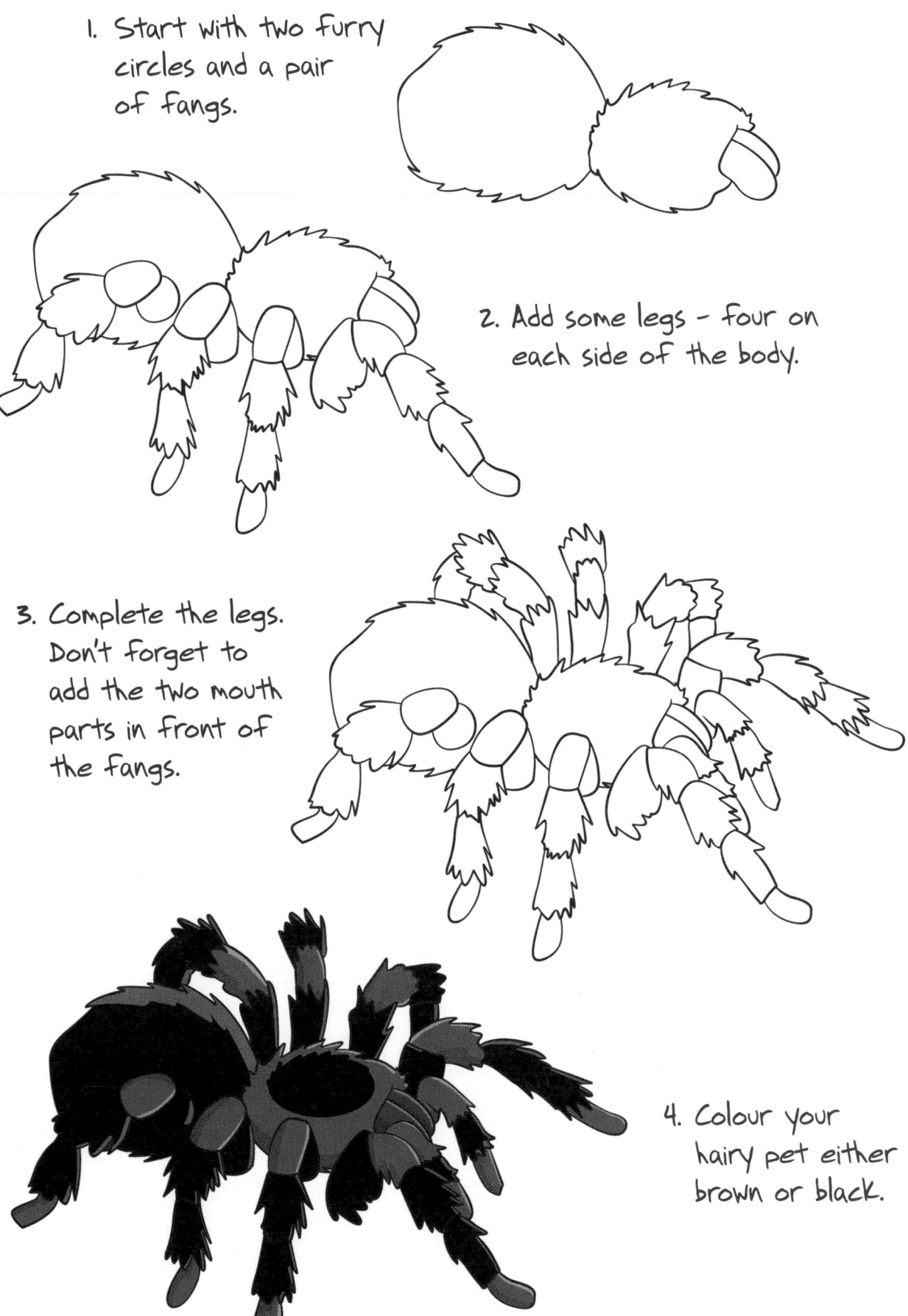

2. Add some legs - four on each side of the body.

3. Complete the legs. Don't forget to add the two mouth parts in front of the fangs.

4. Colour your hairy pet either brown or black.

Chameleon

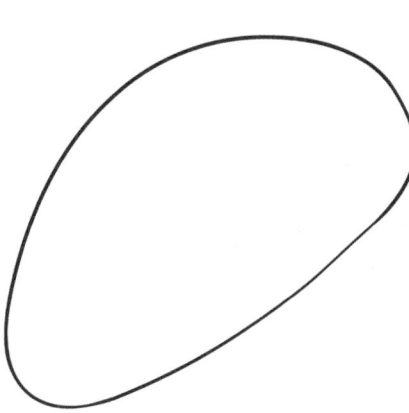

1. Begin with an egg shape for the body.

2. Add a curly tail and a head with a big round eye.

3. This lizard has short legs with gripping toes, and a wide, smiley mouth.

4. Colour him brightly. You could show your chameleon changing from one colour to another to match his surroundings.

Mouse

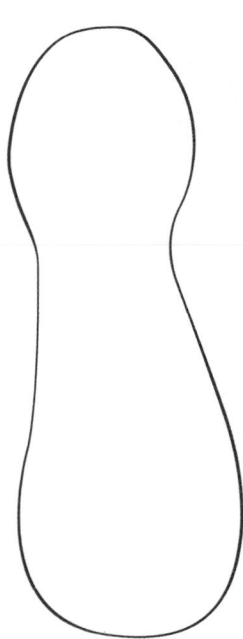

1. Draw this squashed oval shape.

2. Add two big ears and a little face.

3. The legs are next.

4. Colour it in, and don't forget the whiskers.

Parrot

1. Start with this distorted oval shape.

2. Add a curved beak, beady eye and a wing.

3. Draw the bird's feet and a branch for it to stand on.

4. A long pointed tail and lots of bright colours complete the picture.

Kitten

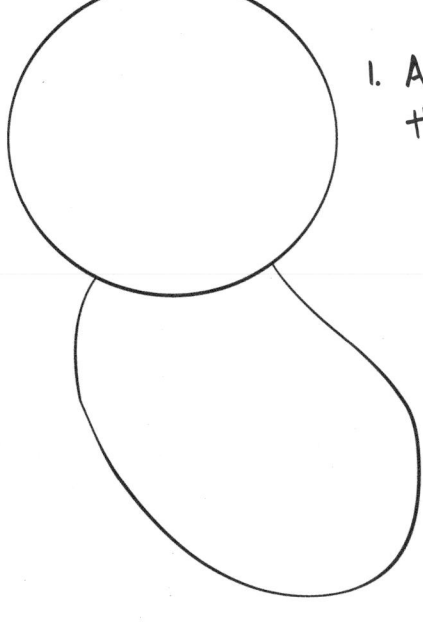

1. A circle and an oval make the head and body.

2. Ears and a cute face are next.

3. Add short legs and dainty feet to your furry friend.

4. You can colour the kitten like this one, or any colour you like.

Frog

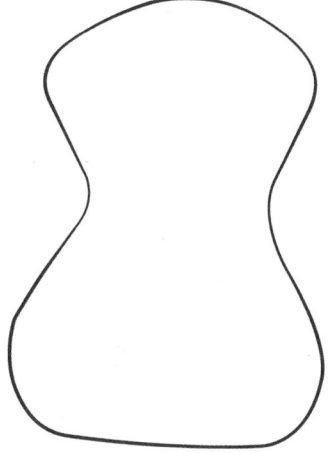

1. Start with a squashed oval.

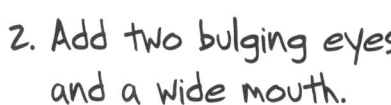

2. Add two bulging eyes and a wide mouth.

3. Add large back legs for jumping, and smaller front legs to keep him steady.

4. Colour your frog green, or brownish-green.

Pony

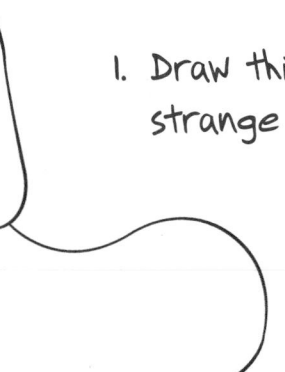

1. Draw this strange shape.

2. Add a face, ears, a long, flowing mane and two legs.

3. Complete all four of the pony's legs.

4. You can make your pony a palomino, like this one, with a pale mane and tail, or maybe skewbald – brown and white.

Cockatoo

1. This shape looks a bit like a trowel.

2. Add a curved beak and a plume of feathers to the head.

3. Wings and legs are next.

4. Colour it white, not forgetting that spectacular yellow plume.

Goat

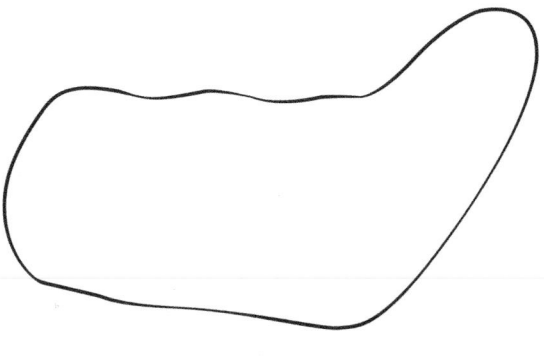

1. Start with the body and neck.

2. Draw a jagged outline to make the body look hairy.

3. Finish off the legs and draw in the horns.

4. Use grey, brown or black to colour in your groovy goat.

Guinea Pig

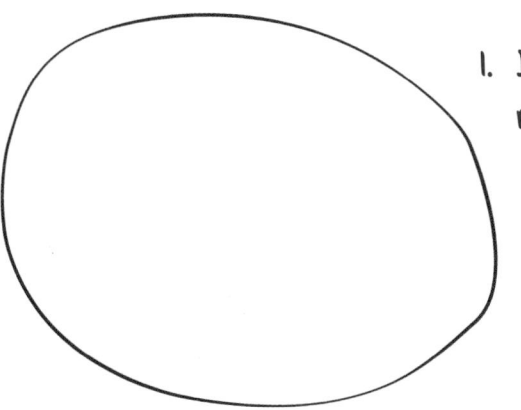

1. Draw this slightly mis-shapen circle.

2. Add the head, ears and one of the legs.

3. Now draw a smiley face and another leg.

4. Add some whiskers and the back legs, then colour in your picture.

Tropical Fish

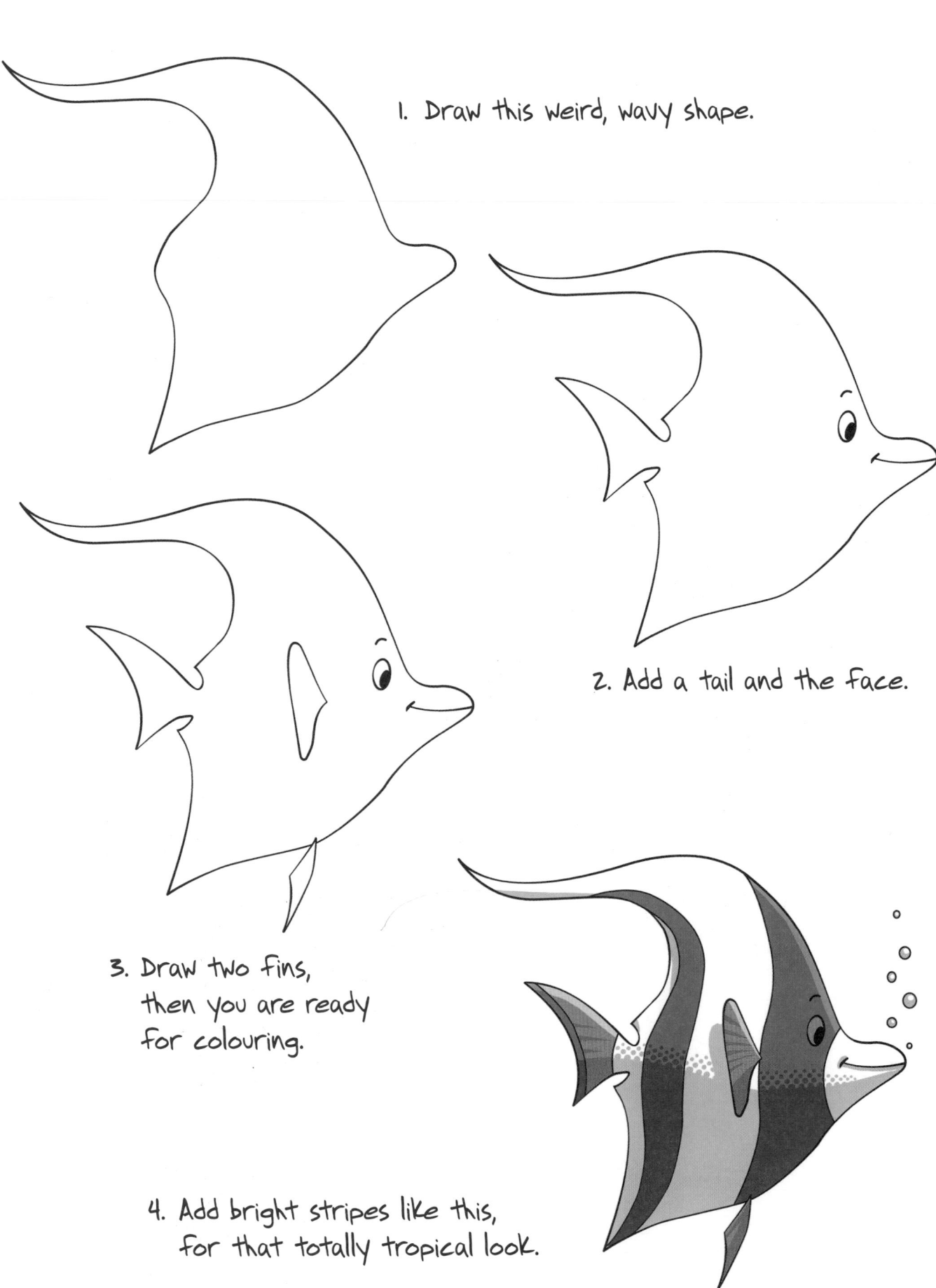

1. Draw this weird, wavy shape.

2. Add a tail and the face.

3. Draw two fins, then you are ready for colouring.

4. Add bright stripes like this, for that totally tropical look.

Dove

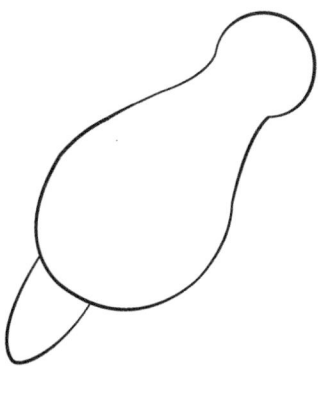

1. Begin with the body and one of the legs.

2. Add the wings and a beak.

3. Add feathers to the wings and tail using these long, finger shapes.

4. Doves are white, so shading plays an important part in the colouring.

PUPPY

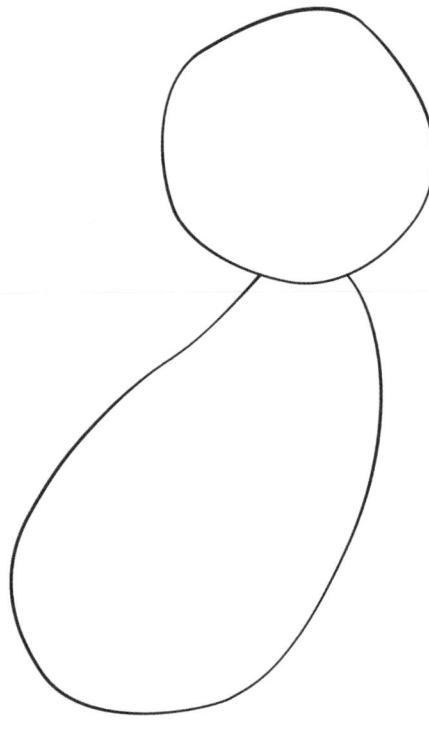

1. A squashed oval and a circle make the head and body.

2. Add the ears, face and a round, shiny nose.

3. Draw the legs next.

4. Add your puppy's tail, and colour him in.

Ferret

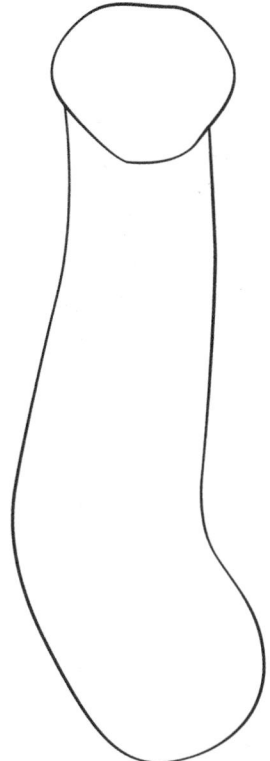

1. Draw a sausage shape and a circle for the body and head.

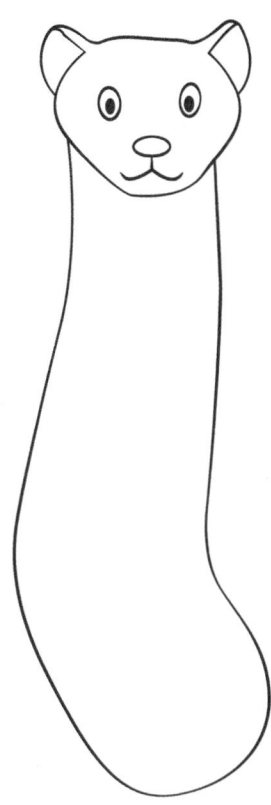

2. Now draw the ears and face.

3. Long front legs and short strong back ones help it to burrow.

4. Colour in your ferret – any shade of brown will do.

Snake

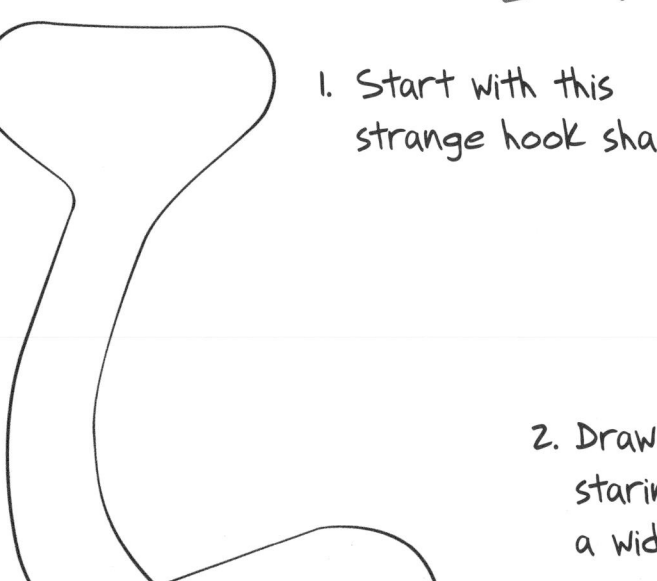

1. Start with this strange hook shape.

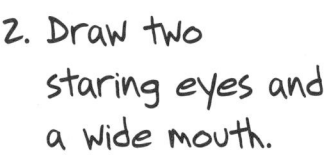

2. Draw two staring eyes and a wide mouth.

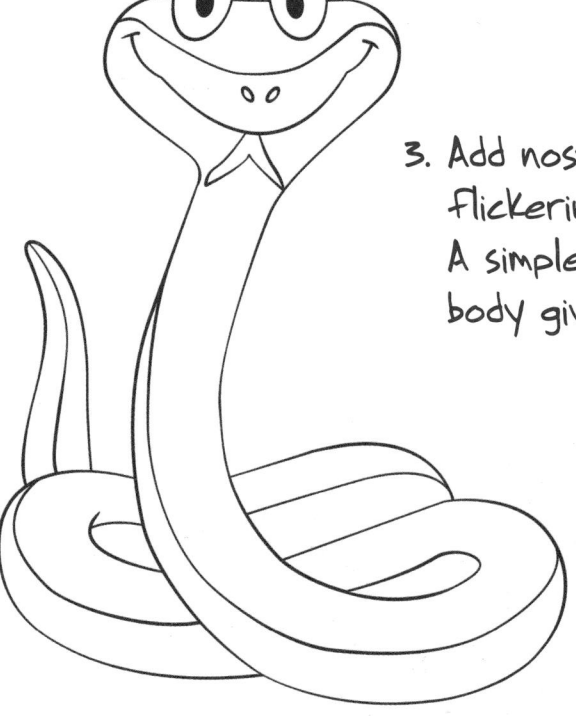

3. Add nostrils and a flickering tongue. A simple line along the body gives it shape.

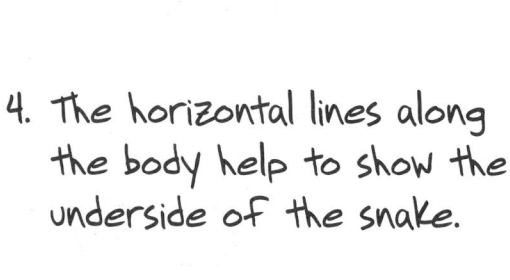

4. The horizontal lines along the body help to show the underside of the snake.

Rabbit

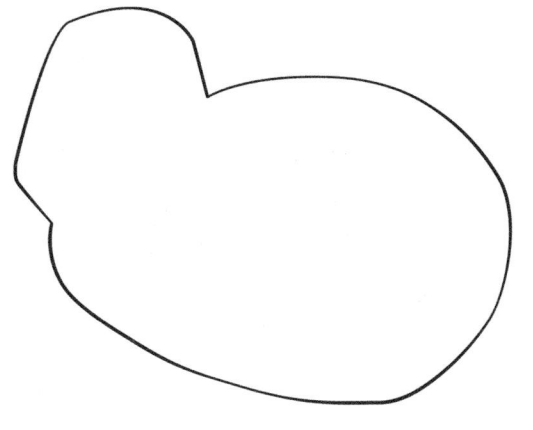

1. Draw an oval shape and add a bulge on one side.

2. Next draw the ears and the face, with some big bunny teeth.

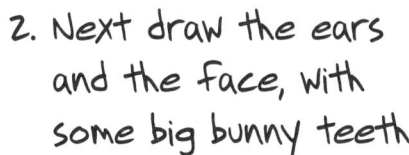

3. Add short front legs and powerful back legs – good for hopping.

4. Add some whiskers and a fluffy tail, then you are ready for colouring.

Space

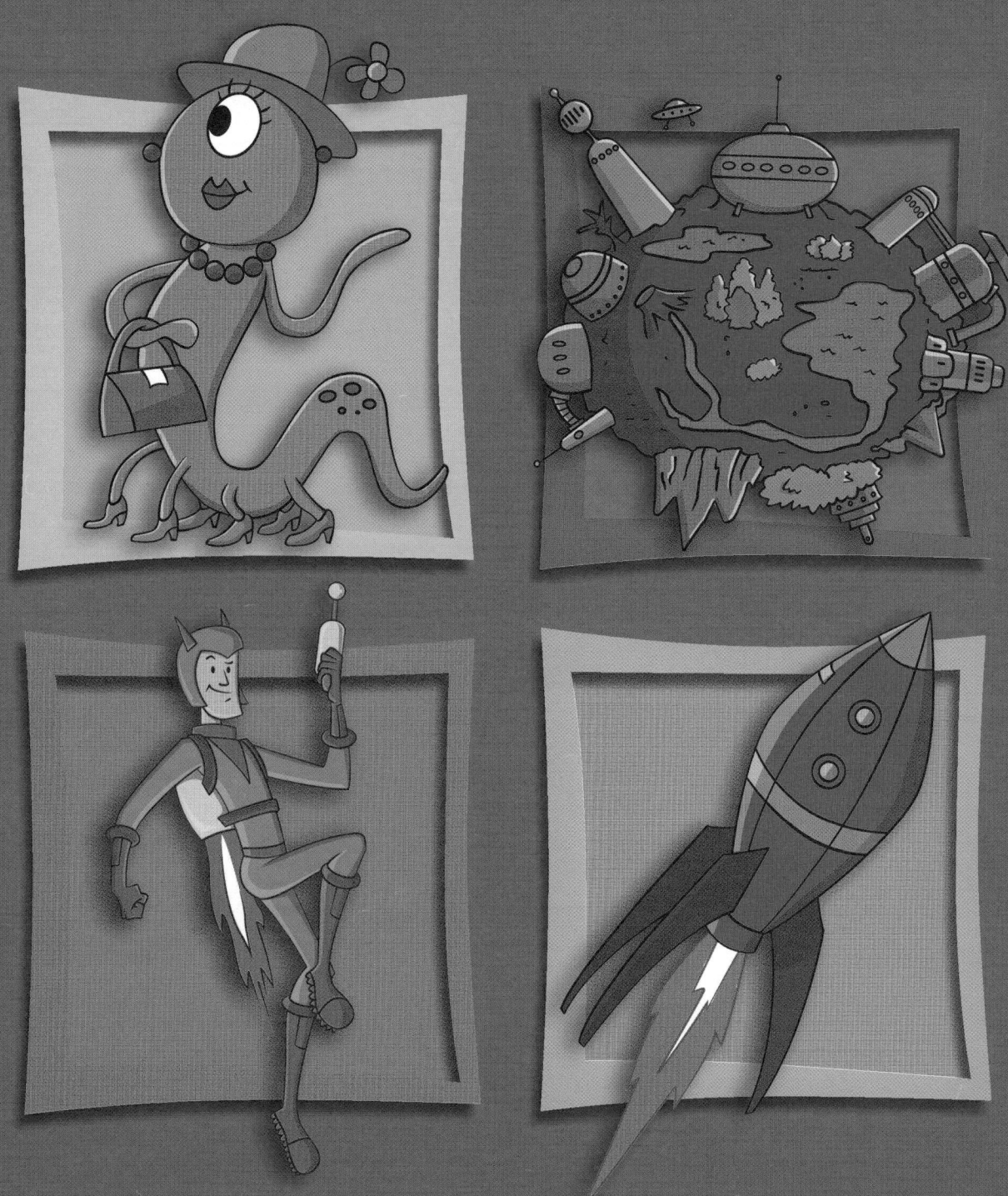

Alien Mum

1. Draw a shape like a wriggly worm for the body, with a circle for the head.

2. Add lots of legs and wriggly arms just like her body.

3. Give her a fancy hat and, of course, lots of pretty shoes.

4. Add a handbag, jewellery and some lipstick, and this mum is ready to face the world!

Alien Dad

1. A large blob shape makes up the body and head.

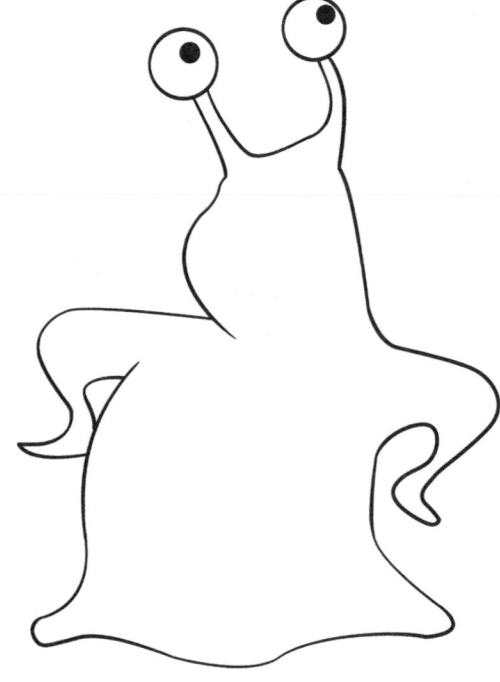

2. Draw eyes on stalks and two bendy arms.

3. Don't forget his "cool" dad shirt.

4. Colour him in bright green with red splodges to match his shirt!

Alien Son

1. Start with this strange shape.

2. Add an eye and two more legs.

3. Give your alien boy a baseball cap and a ball to play with.

4. Add one tooth and colour him in brightly.

Alien Daughter

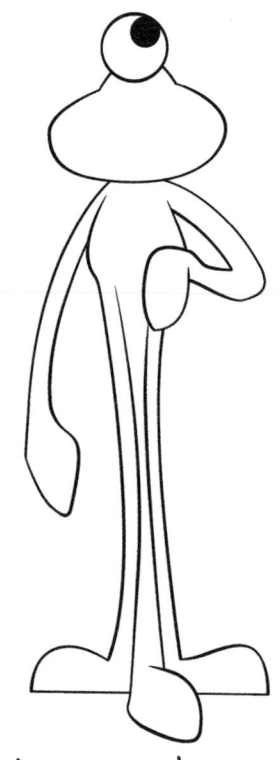

1. This strange, long thin shape makes the body and head.

2. An extra leg in the middle, a single eye and floppy arms make her look more alien.

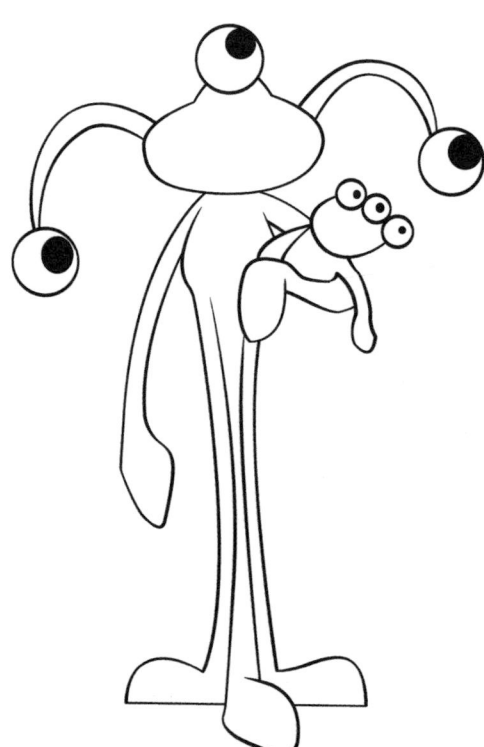

3. Add some tentacles and give her more eyes.

4. Colour her however you want – and don't forget the cuddly toy.

Alien Pet

1. This lumpy-bumpy shape makes the body.

2. Add five eyes so that he can see all around.

3. Stubby little legs and a funny tail are next.

4. Add a tongue and bristly hairs on his back to finish.

UFO

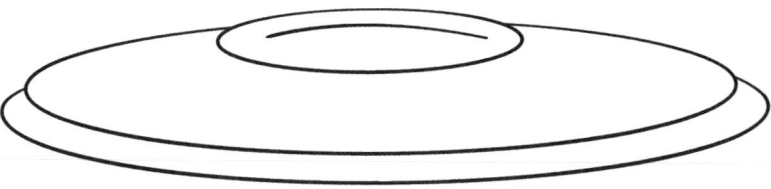

1. A collection of circles gives you the basic shape.

2. Next add a dome and a friendly-looking alien.

3. Give the alien arms to control the UFO and for waving at people.

4. Add some legs and lights to the UFO, then get to work with your colours.

Space Warrior

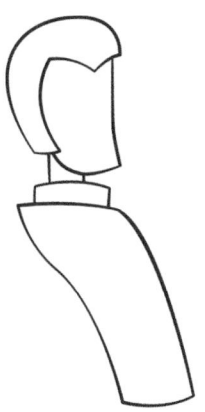

1. Start with a curved back to make your warrior look as though he's moving.

2. Draw his arms in an action-packed pose.

3. One knee up in the air shows he's leaping off the ground.

4. Finish him off by adding a powerful jet pack and a cool zap gun!

Alien Planet

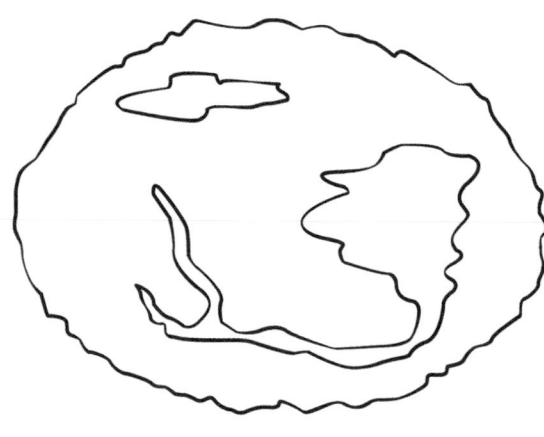

1. Draw this wobbly circle shape.

2. Add some strange buildings sticking out of the land.

3. Draw some forests and volcanoes to add interest.

4. Colour any way you want – the stranger the better!

Earth

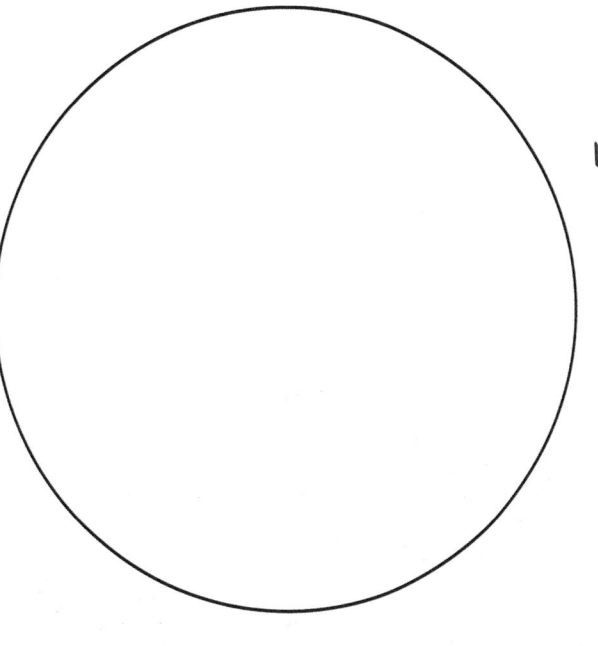

1. Draw a circle to start with.

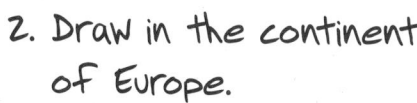

2. Draw in the continent of Europe.

3. You need to show Africa on this part of the globe, so add this continent too.

4. Colour the land mass green. Remember – use plenty of blue for all the water that makes up our planet.

Mars Rover

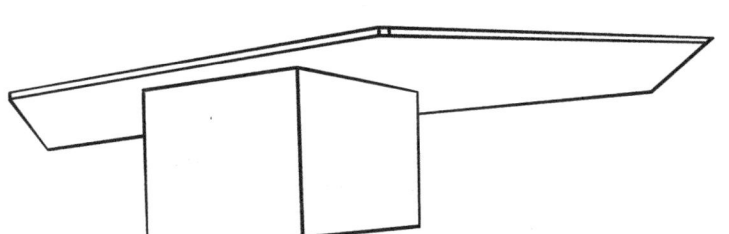

1. Start with a cube and draw a flat panel on top.

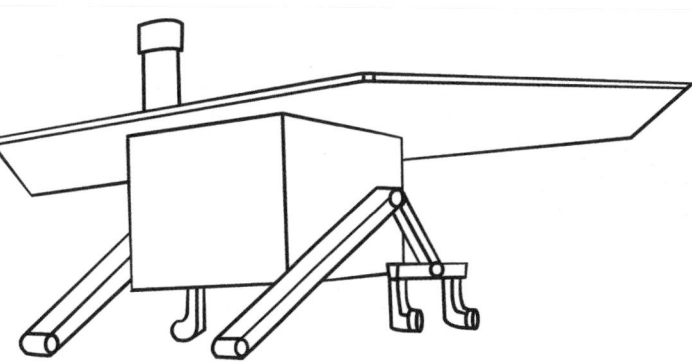

2. Add the leg struts and the pole.

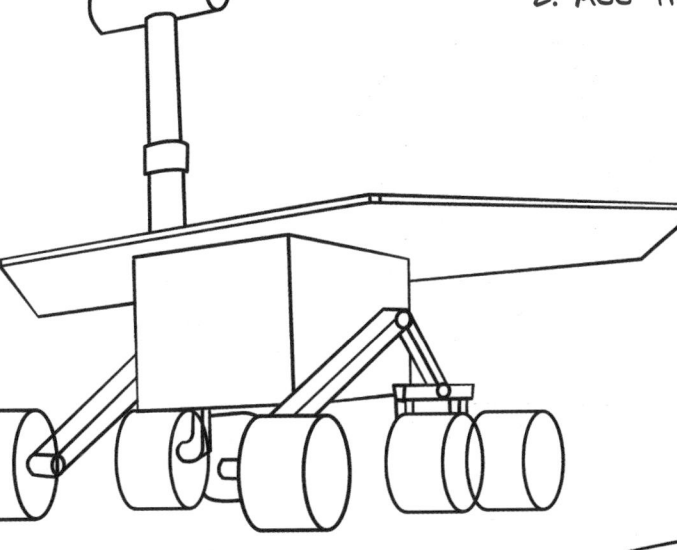

3. Draw some wheels, and a sensor unit on top of the pole.

4. Lights and aerials help the rover to communicate and find its way around.

Alien Car

1. Start with this long, flattened oval shape.

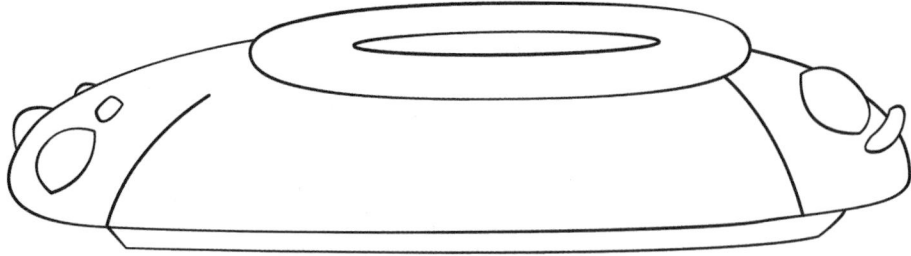

2. Add lights at the front and back, and draw a hole for the driver to sit in.

3. A glass cover helps protect the driver from the intergalactic weather.

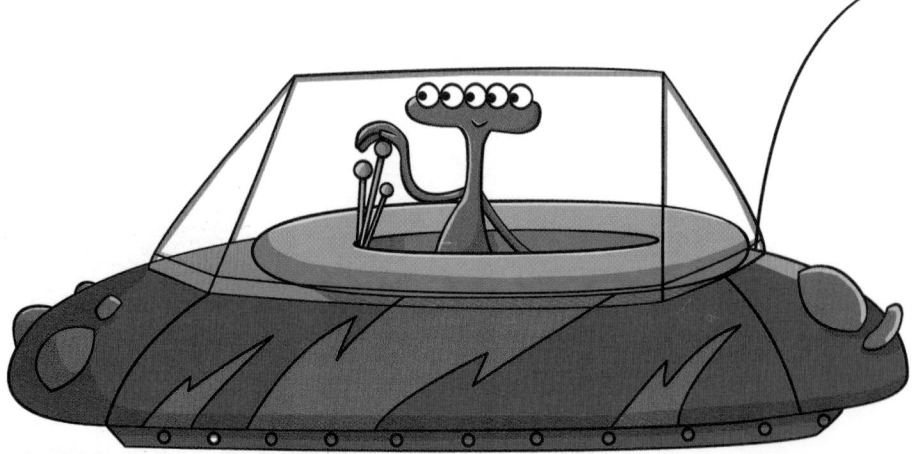

4. Give it a sporty paint job.

Moon Base

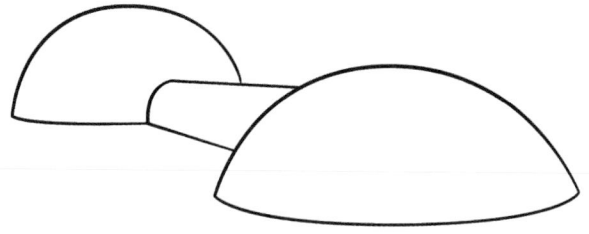

1. Two half circles
   connected by a tube
   form the main base.

2. Add more tubes to
   create different
   areas of the base.

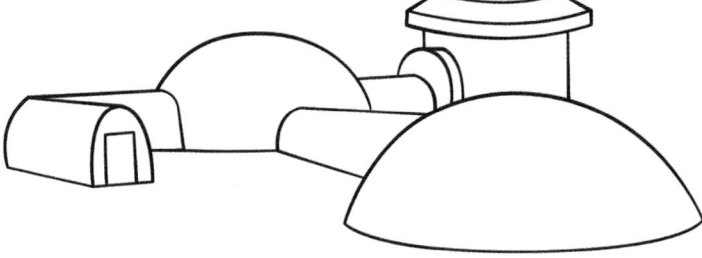

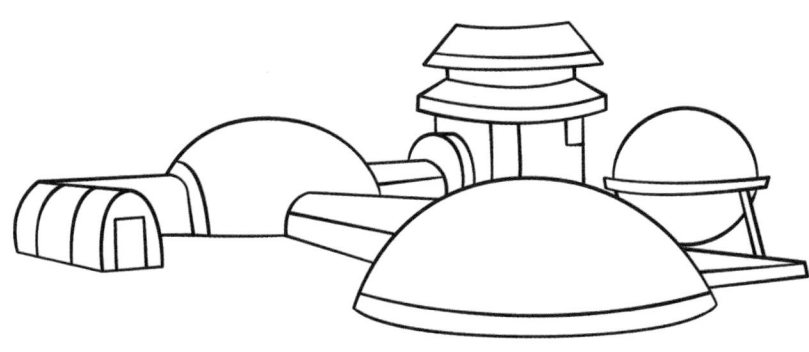

3. A tower and a circular
   storage dome give
   added interest.

4. Add criss-cross lines to
   the connecting tubes to
   make them look like glass.

Saturn

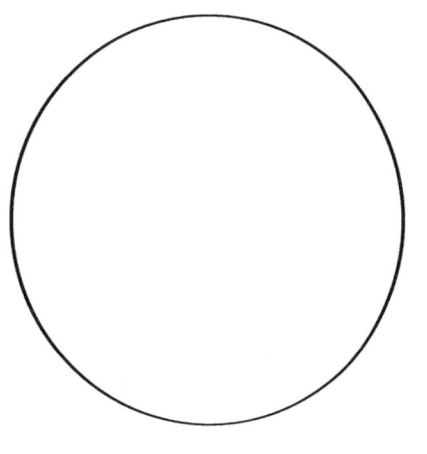

1. Start with a circle.

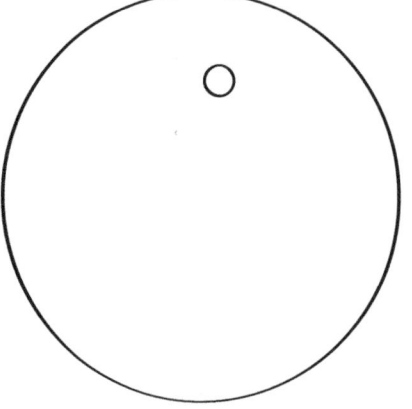

2. Add the spot on the planet and a couple of moons circling it.

3. Saturn wouldn't look right without its rings.

4. Paint your planet the famous pale orange colour.

Rocket

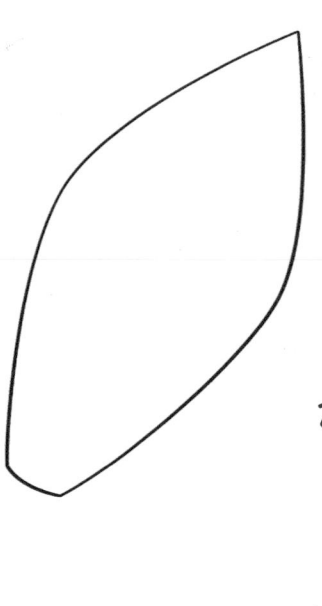

1. Draw this pointed teardrop shape.

2. Add three fins – these help the rocket in flight and work as legs for landing too.

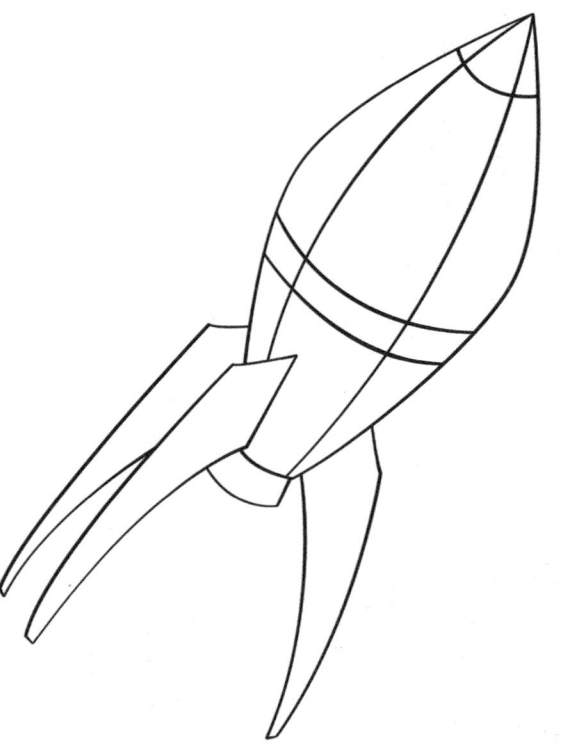

3. A large booster nozzle on the base makes the rocket look powerful.

4. Don't forget to add windows and plenty of flames shooting out of the booster nozzle.

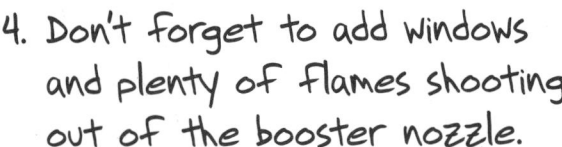

Space Station

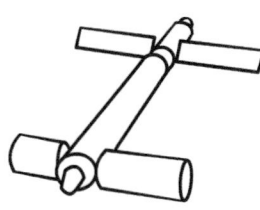

1. A collection of tubes starts everything off.

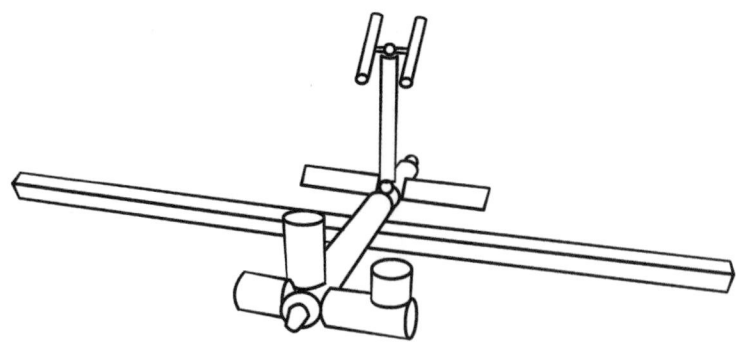

2. Add some struts and more tubes.

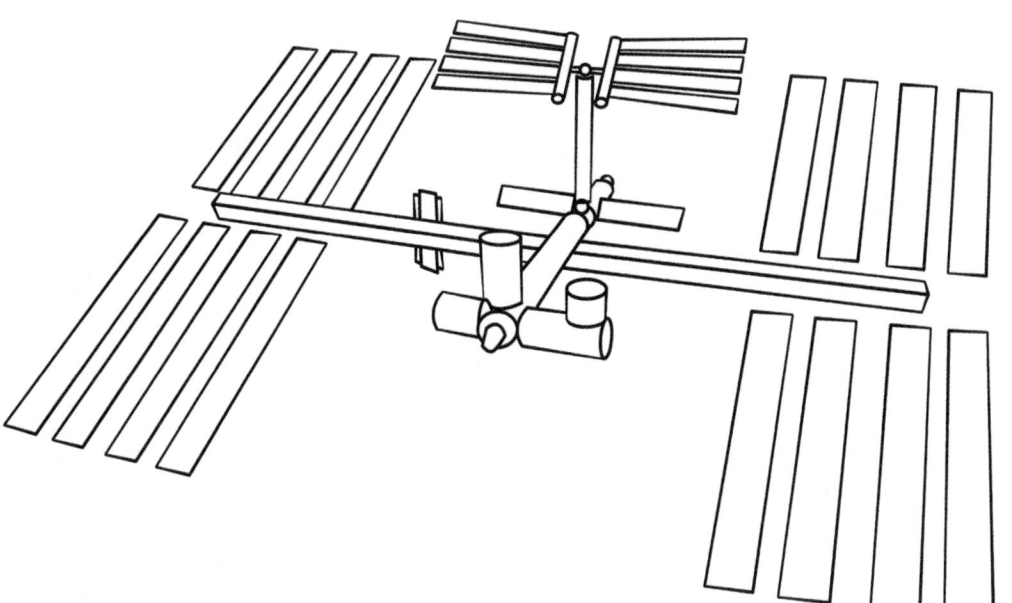

3. Add lots of flat solar panels to help provide power.

4. Use shades of grey to make it look metallic. Now this space station is ready to orbit the Earth.

Vehicles

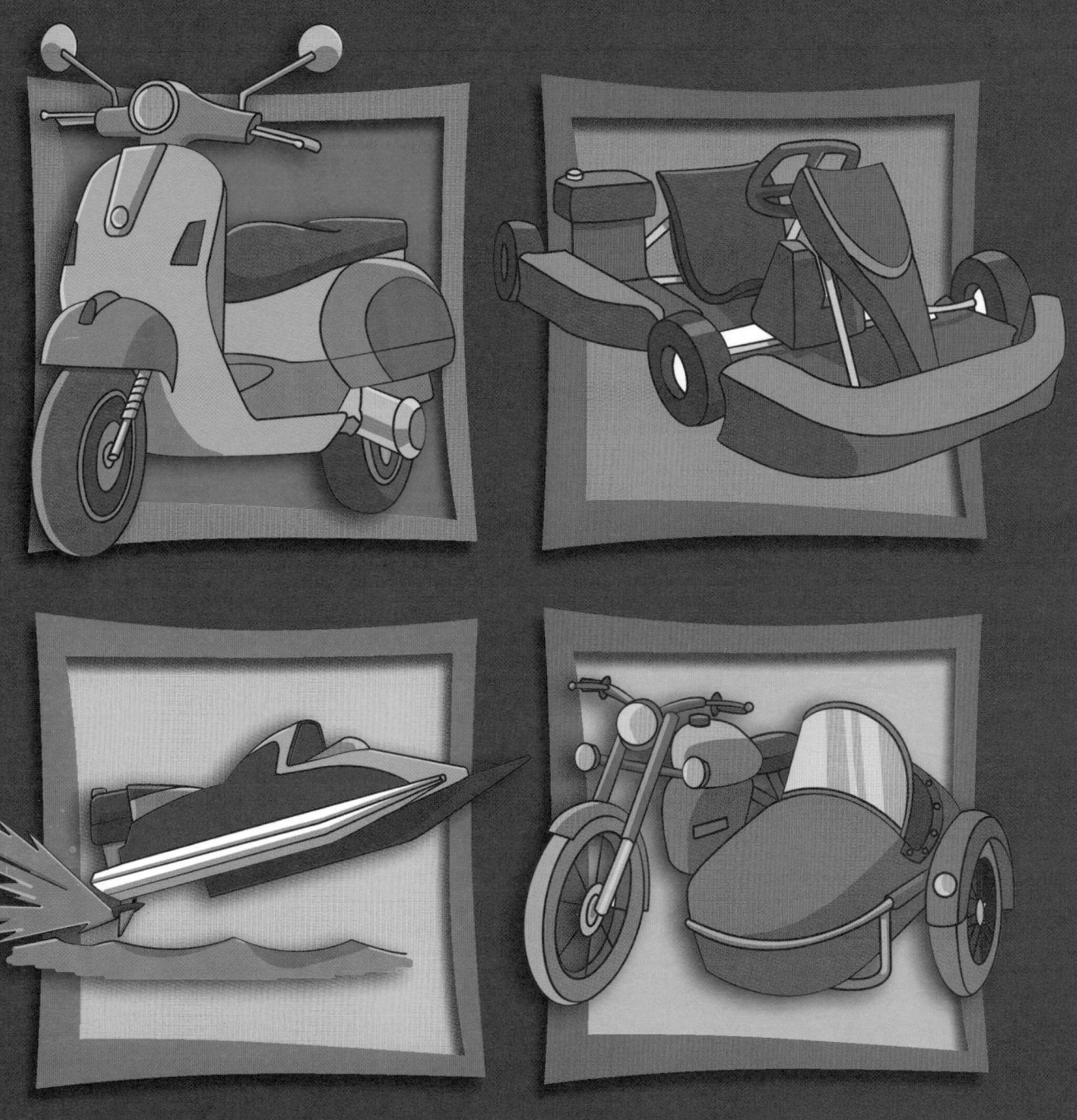

Jet Powerboat

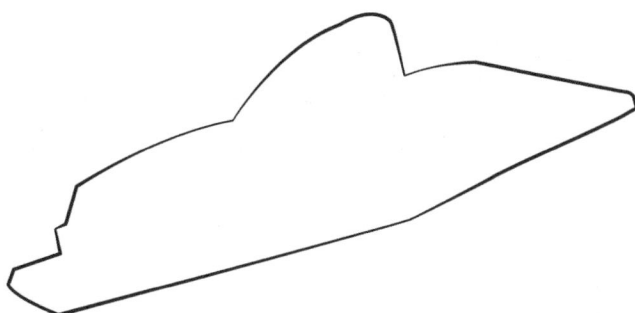

1. Start with this angular shape.

2. Add detailing lines to show the edges of the boat.

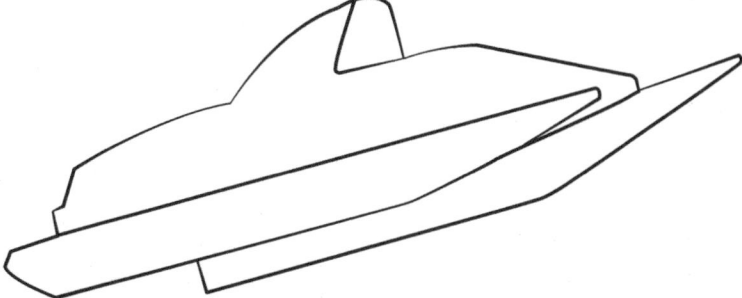

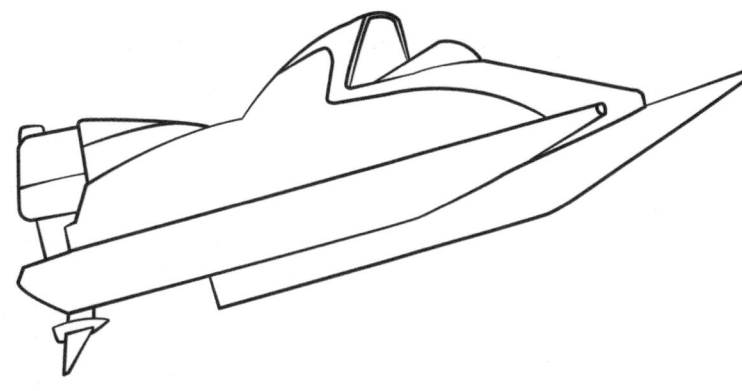

3. Draw the engine at the back and the cockpit glass at the front.

4. Leave a gap between the boat and the water to make it look as though it's leaping through the waves.

Dumper Truck

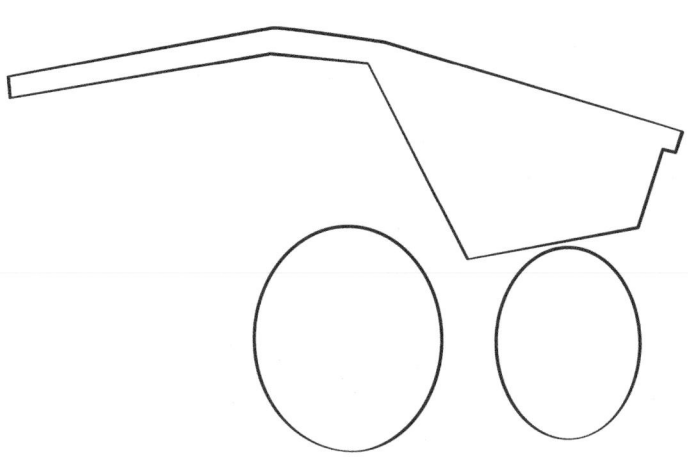

1. Draw two circles for the wheels and a cart-shape for the main body.

2. Next add the cab and an engine at the front.

3. Draw in the rest of the body and add an upright exhaust.

4. Colour it in – yellow is best.

Go Kart

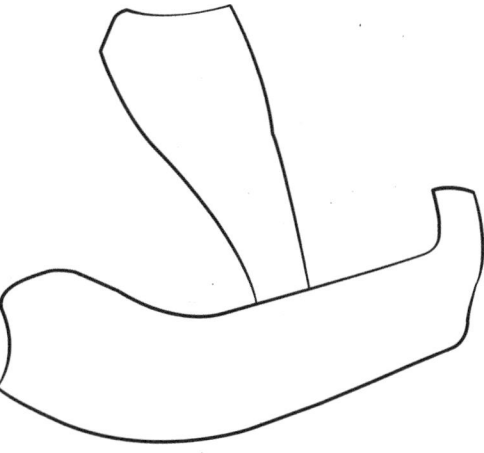

1. These shapes make up the front bumper and steering column.

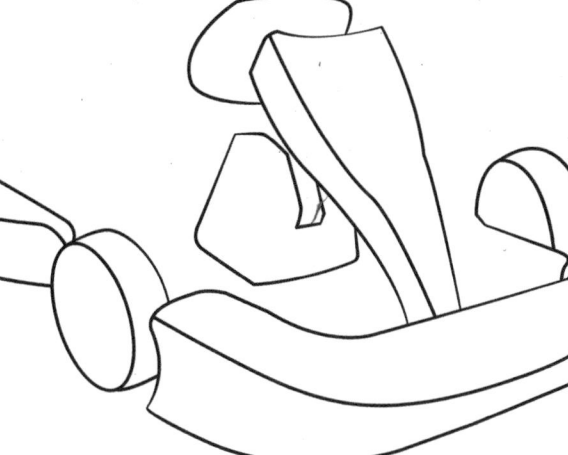

2. Draw in the wheels – you can only see three from this angle. Add the steering wheel.

3. Add the seat and fuel tank and give the steering wheel some more detail.

4. Colour it in go-faster red and black.

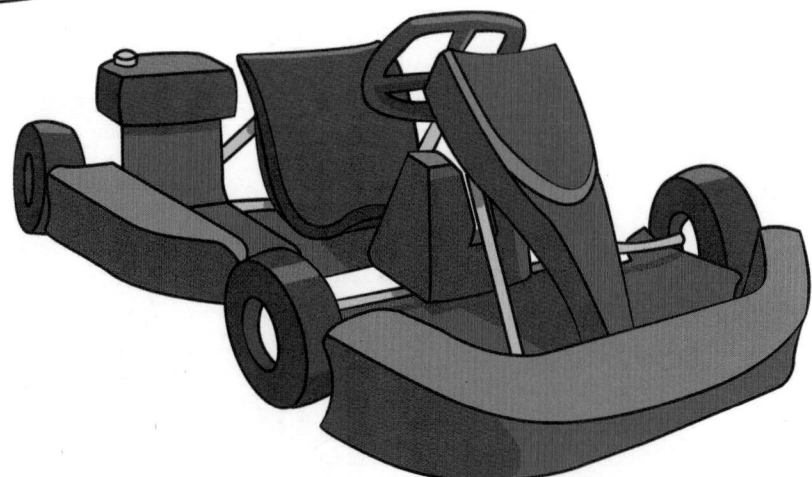

Hot-air Balloon

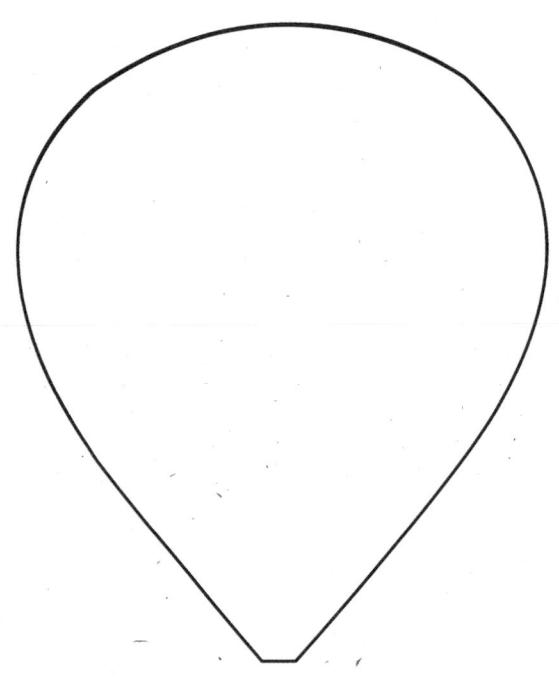

1. Start with a huge upside-down teardrop shape.

2. Draw the basket and ropes below.

3. Add stripes to the balloon to help give it shape.

4. Colour your balloon brightly. Don't forget a burner to make it float!

Four-wheel Drive

1. Start with a shape that looks a bit like a sofa.

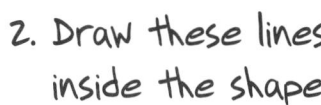

2. Draw these lines inside the shape.

3. Add the wheels and the headlights. Include some more line detail on the body.

4. Colour it green for an off-road, country feel.

Segway

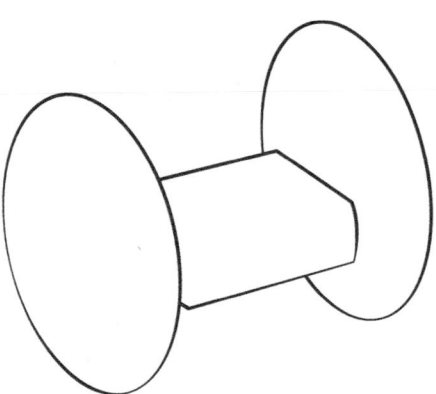

1. Start with two circles and a rectangle.

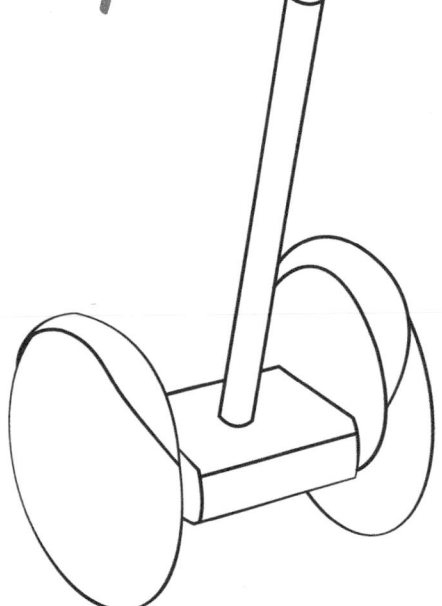

2. Draw the main control stick, and guards for the wheels.

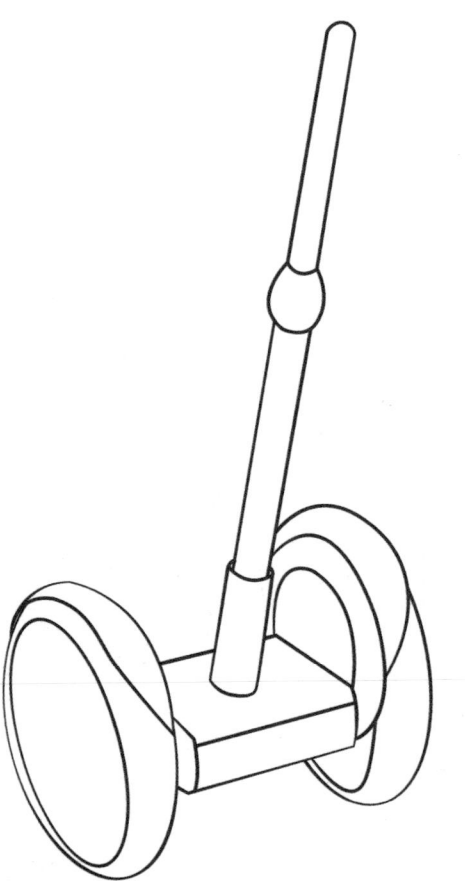

3. Add more line detail to the wheels and control stick.

4. Finish it by adding the handlebars and colour.

Scooter

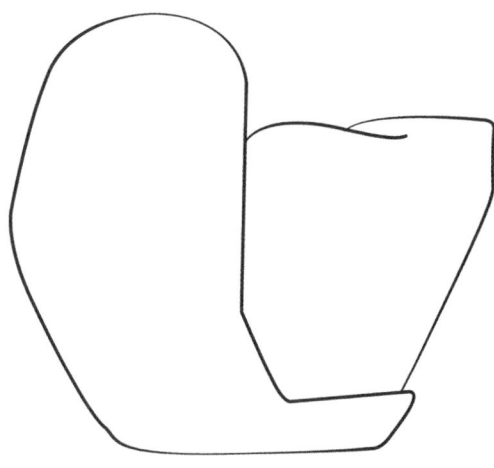

1. Start with this strange shape.

2. Draw a line to define the seat. Add a steering column and mudguards.

3. Follow this with handlebars, wheels and more line detail to the body.

4. Before scooting off, add lights, mirrors, and colour it in.

Hovercraft

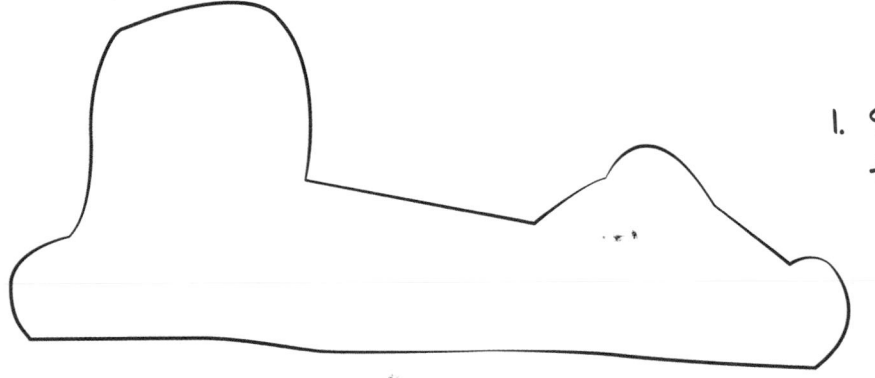

1. Start with this shape.

2. Add a teardrop shape for the centre of the fan, then draw the main hoverskirt.

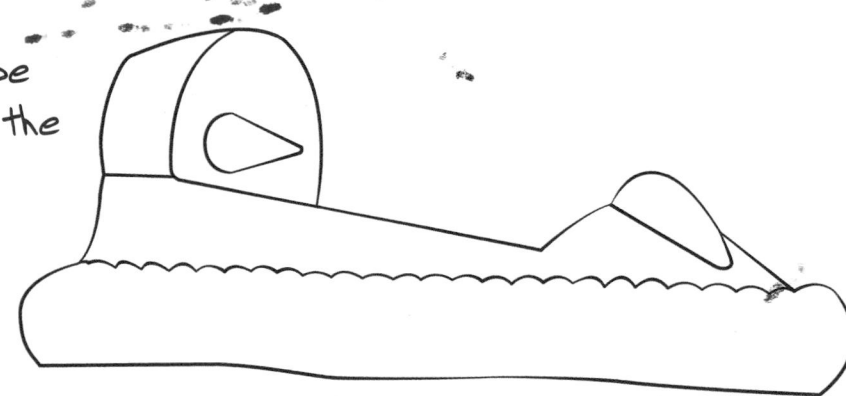

3. Draw in fan blades, handlebars and a screen for the driver.

4. Be sure to colour the skirt differently from the rest of the vehicle to make it stand out.

Motorbike

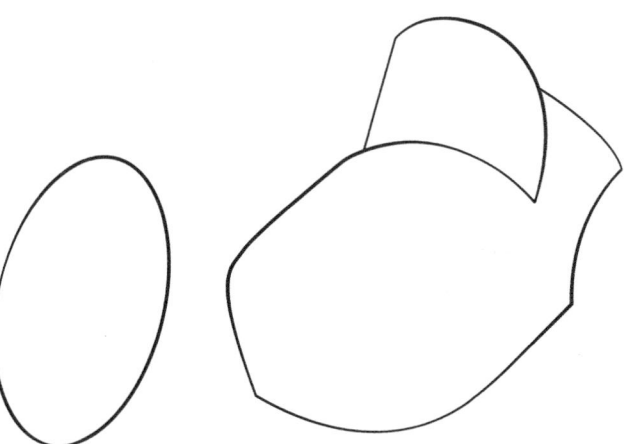

1. Use these shapes to start the drawing of your motorbike with sidecar.

2. Begin to build up the bike, drawing the petrol tank. Add a wheel to the sidecar.

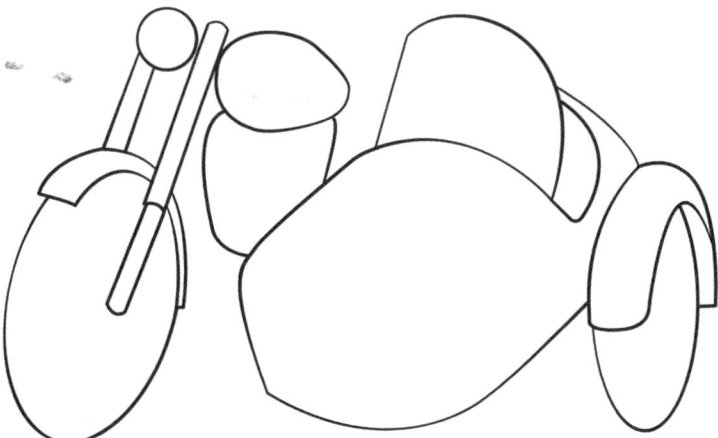

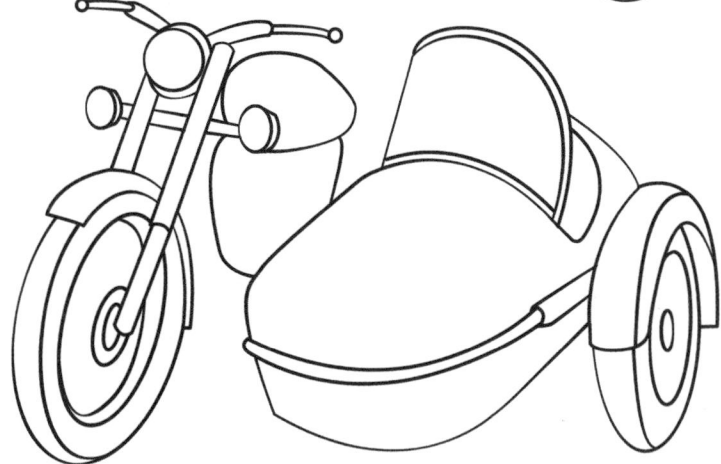

3. The inclusion of lights and handlebars almost completes the bike.

4. Fill in the rest of the bike frame and add your colour.

Army Helicopter

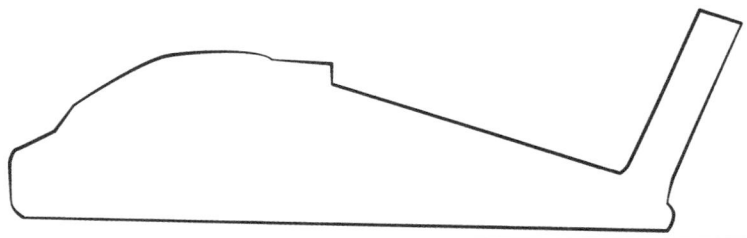

1. Draw the outline of the main body first.

2. Draw the tail rotor, then add the other details you see here.

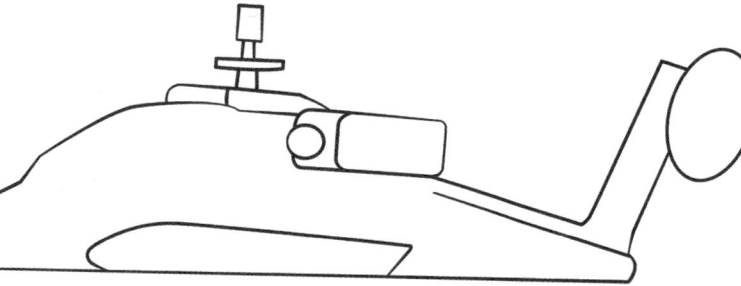

3. Add the main rotor blade, then the cockpit and some weaponry.

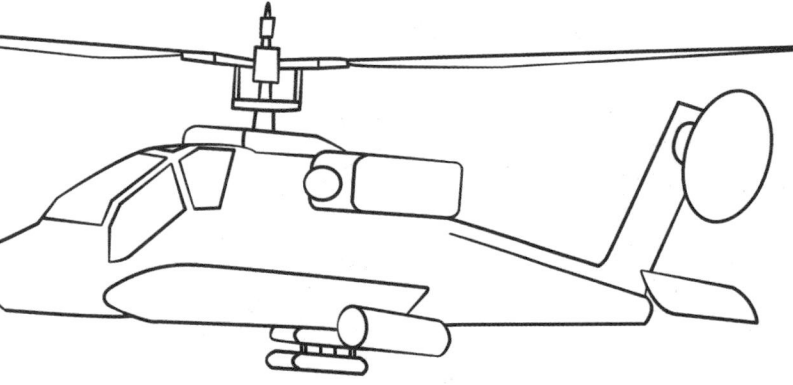

4. Colour it however you want – green will make it look like a real army vehicle.

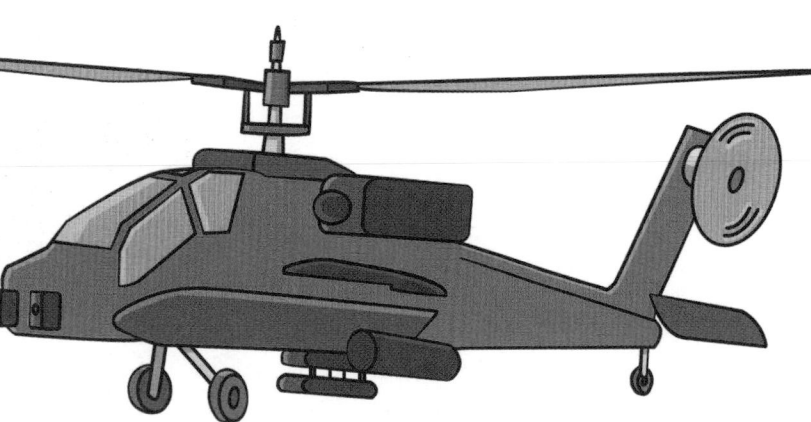

Monster Truck

1. This is the main body of the truck.

2. Add some wheels and windows.

3. Add huge, chunky treads on the tyres, and a searchlight.

4. Finish off the main body frame – don't forget the painted-on flames to make it look cool.

Steam Train

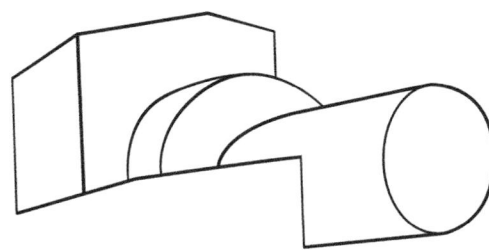

1. Start with this assortment of cylinders and blocks.

2. Add more blocks for the tender - the fuel truck right behind the engine.

3. Draw more blocks for the rest of the trucks, and add circles for the wheels.

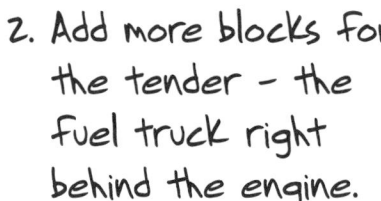

4. Add buffers at the front. Now colour it in.

Eco Car

1. This odd, curved shape is your starting point.

2. Add a windscreen and mudguards.

3. Draw the windows and wheels.

4. Finish the inside by adding seats. Colour the car green, or another smart shade.

Stunt Plane

1. Start with a curved body and nose cone.

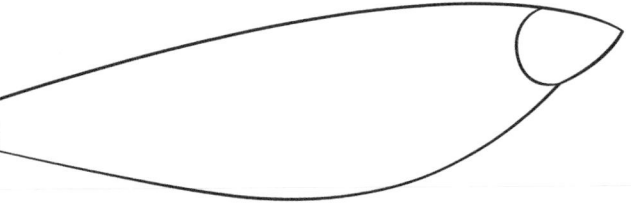

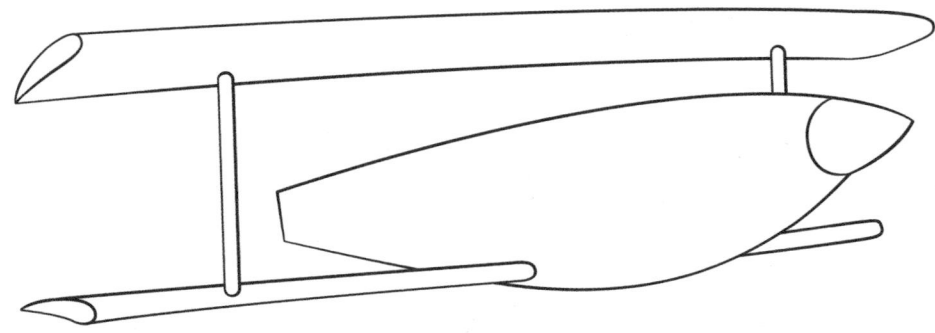

2. The two wings are placed one above the other, and held together with struts.

3. The wheels on the end of the legs are covered when the plane is flying.

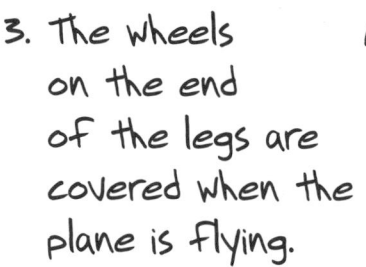

4. Add a propeller. Remember – no stunt plane is complete without plenty of flames painted on!

Sports Car

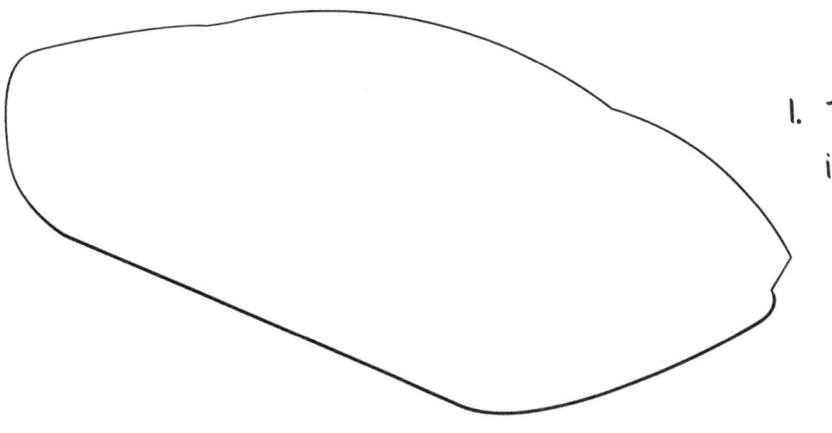

1. This distorted rectangle is your first step.

2. Now add windows and a grill at the front. Remember to leave a space for the wheels.

3. Simple lines define the bonnet and doors.

4. Add some lights. Use colour to separate the bumpers from the rest of the body.

Toys

Teddy Bear

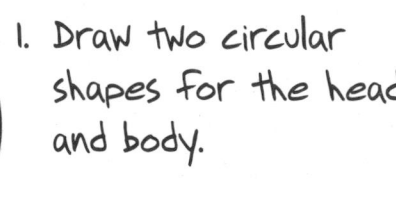

1. Draw two circular shapes for the head and body.

2. Add more circles to make the feet and nose. Draw two sausage shapes for the arms.

3. Draw two ears and finish off the nose and face.

4. Add some little lines to look like stitching.

Action Figure

1. Start with this jacket shape.

2. Add a head with a helmet. Draw the legs.

3. Next draw some goggles on the helmet and add facial features, hands and feet.

4. Use green and brown colouring to camouflage this action figure when he's in combat.

BMX

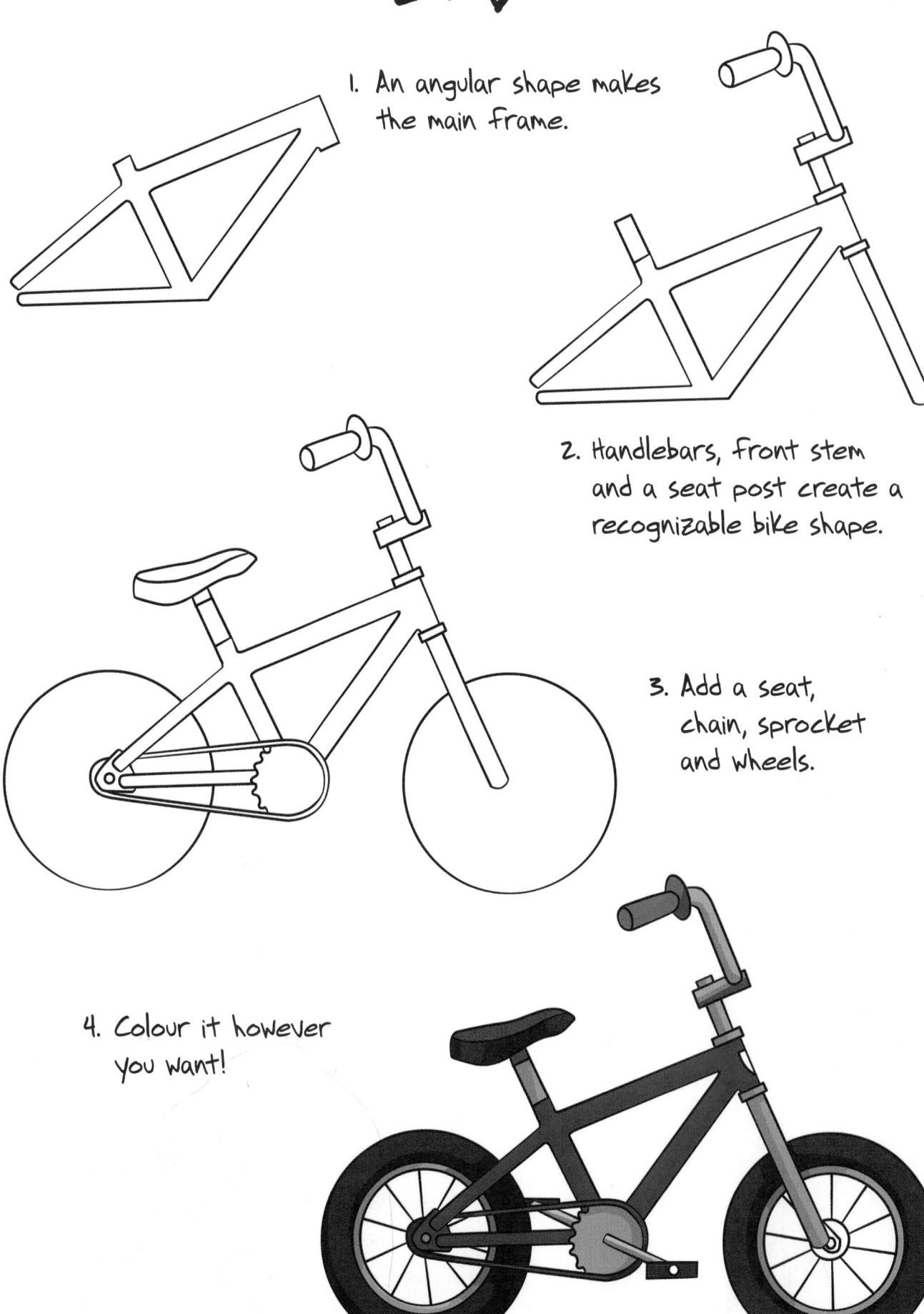

1. An angular shape makes the main frame.

2. Handlebars, front stem and a seat post create a recognizable bike shape.

3. Add a seat, chain, sprocket and wheels.

4. Colour it however you want!

Skateboard

1. A flat shape with a turned-up end starts this easy drawing.

2. Next add four wheels.

3. Now add the trucks and risers.

4. Don't forget to draw some cool designs on the deck when colouring.

Xylophone

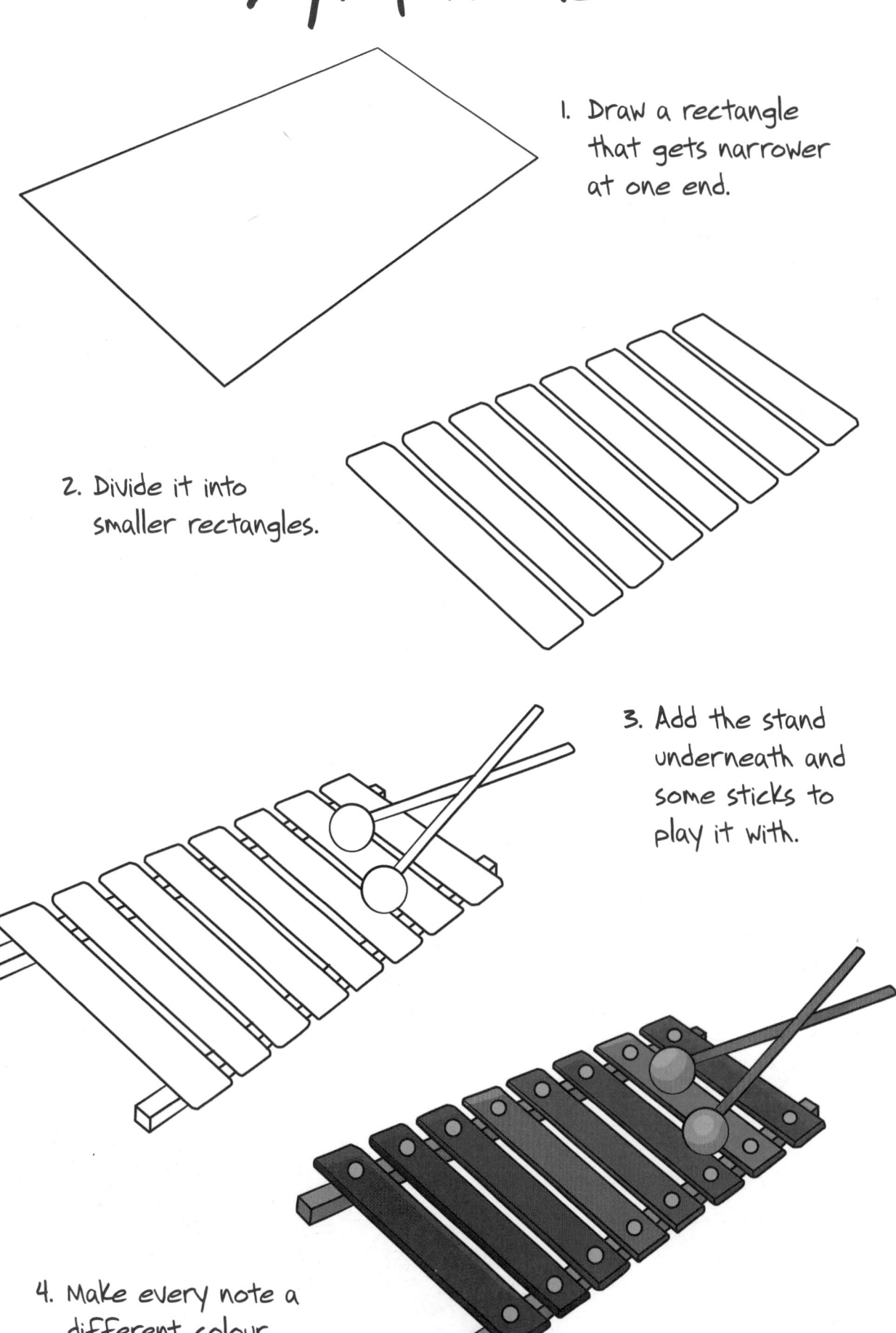

1. Draw a rectangle that gets narrower at one end.

2. Divide it into smaller rectangles.

3. Add the stand underneath and some sticks to play it with.

4. Make every note a different colour.

Doll

1. The body and arms are all one piece in this drawing.

2. Add the pigtails, dress and legs next.

3. Draw the rest of the facial features, plus some detail on the dress.

4. Colour the dress prettily and give the doll stripey tights and rosy cheeks.

Drum Kit

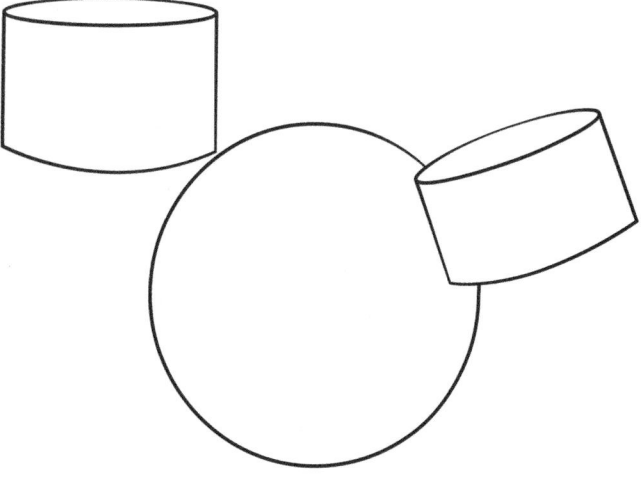

1. A circle and two cylinders form the basis of this drum kit.

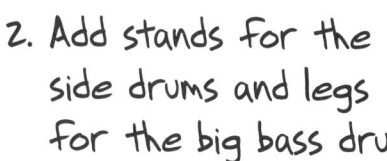

2. Add stands for the side drums and legs for the big bass drum.

3. Add details to make it look like a professional drum kit.

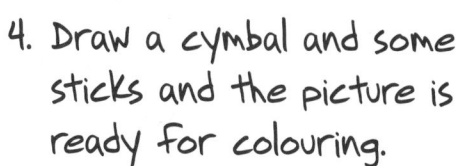

4. Draw a cymbal and some sticks and the picture is ready for colouring.

Electric Guitar

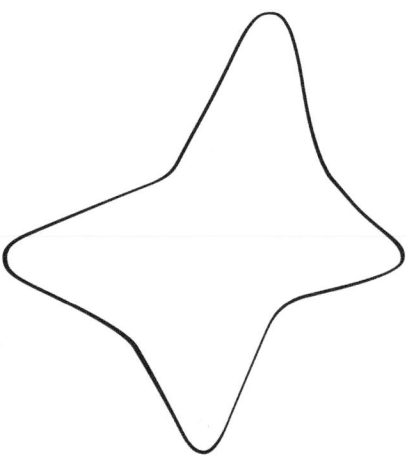

1. This guitar is for a rock star, so begin with a star shape.

2. Draw a long straight neck.

3. Adding lots of buttons to the guitar will make it look cool.

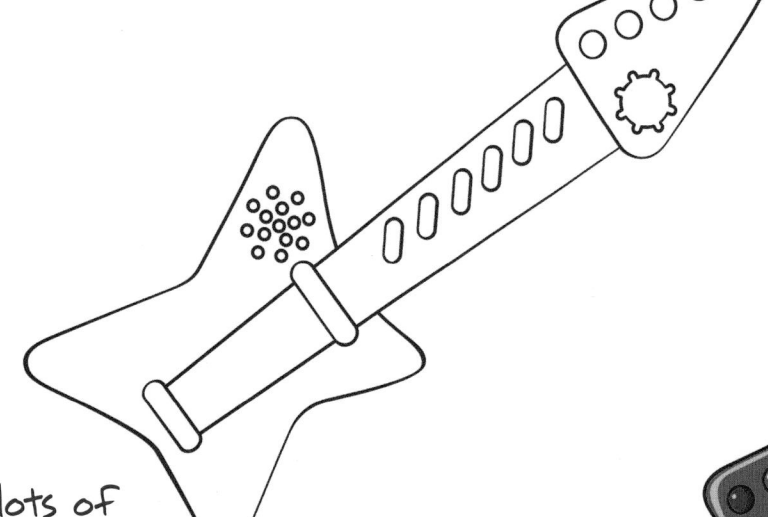

4. Don't forget to add the strings. Now you've got a guitar to be proud of!

Jack-in-the-box

1. Start with a spiky head shape and small body.

2. Add the box and a clown's face.

3. Finish off the clown's costume – don't forget the winder on the box to make him jump!

4. Use bold, bright colours.

Remote-control Car

1. Start with this odd jagged shape.

2. Add the crinkly-edged wheels, a rear spoiler and the driver's cockpit.

3. Add some line detail to the car and draw a box for the controls.

4. Finish off the controls and colour the picture in.

Robot

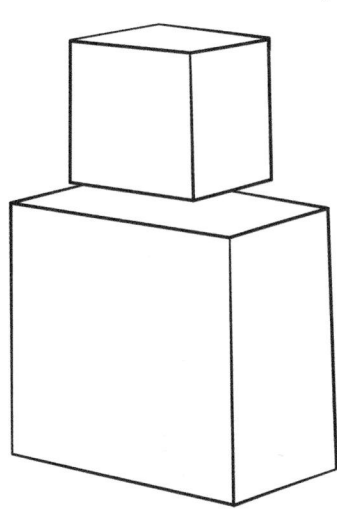

1. Use one large and one small cube for the body and head.

2. Add rectangles for the legs, and circles for the eyes.

3. Add hands to the arms, feet to the legs and finish off the face.

4. Draw plenty of buttons and lights on the front to make him look like a working robot.

Rocking Horse

1. Draw a flat horse outline.

2. Add a curved rocker and a saddle.

3. Draw in the mane and stirrups.

4. Colour it in – remember, most rocking horses are made of wood, so brown is best.

Inline Skates

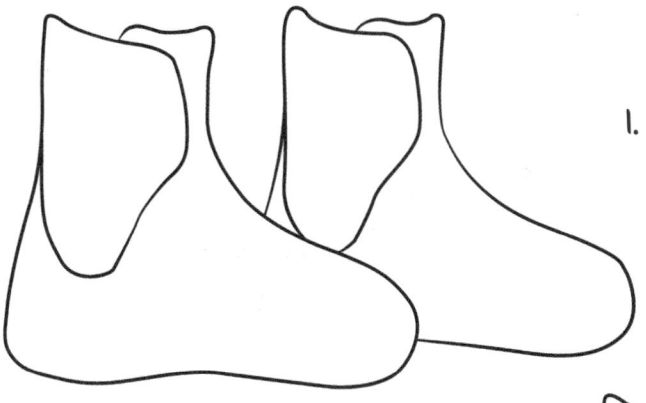

1. Draw these two shapes.

2. Add ankle and foot straps and draw wobbly-looking shapes underneath the boots.

3. Add wheels to the bottom of your drawing.

4. When colouring, don't forget to make the wheels and straps stand out.

Push Scooter

1. These angular shapes make up the main body of the scooter.

2. Add the handlebars and a slot for the back wheel.

3. Draw the wheels in place at the front and back.

4. Colour the main body parts the same, then add contrasting wheels and handlebars.

Water Cannon

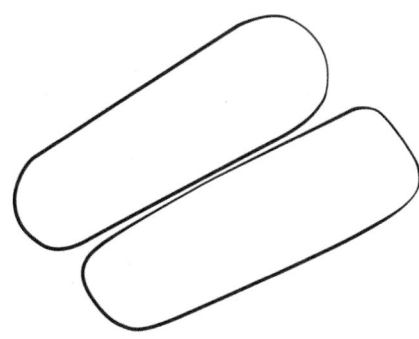

1. Draw two round-cornered rectangles.

2. Add a circle shape at the back and the main nozzle at the front.

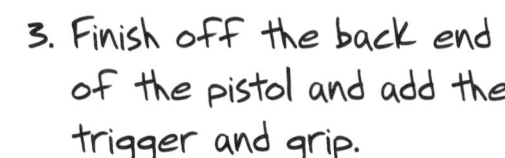

3. Finish off the back end of the pistol and add the trigger and grip.

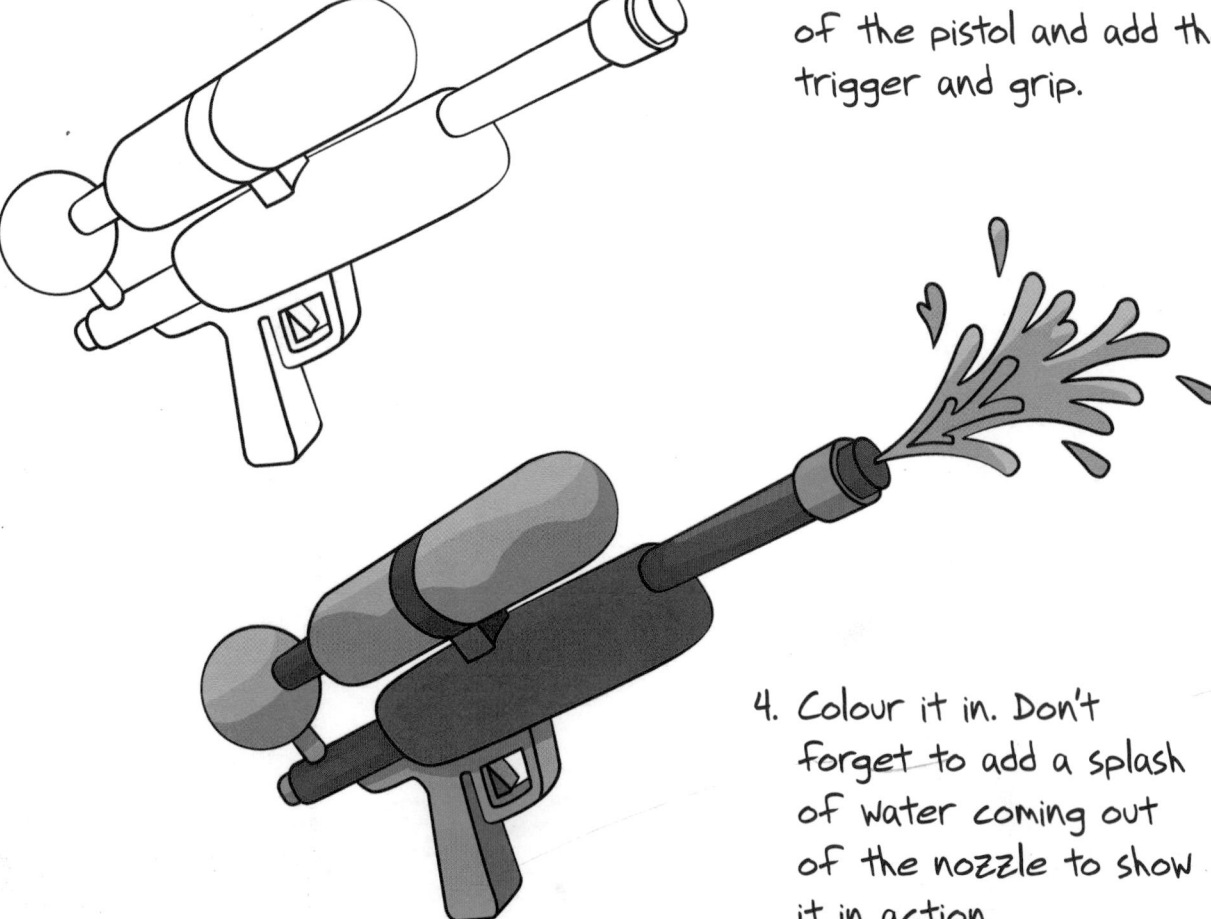

4. Colour it in. Don't forget to add a splash of water coming out of the nozzle to show it in action.